Innovative LibGuides Applications

D1291403

LIBRARY INFORMATION TECHNOLOGY ASSOCIATION (LITA) GUIDES

Marta Mestrovic Deyrup, PhD
Acquisitions Editor, Library Information and Technology Association,
a division of the American Library Association

The Library Information Technology Association (LITA) Guides provide information and guidance on topics related to cutting-edge technology for library and IT specialists.

Written by top professionals in the field of technology, the guides are sought after by librarians wishing to learn a new skill or to become current in today's best practices.

Each book in the series has been overseen editorially since conception by LITA and reviewed by LITA members with special expertise in the specialty area of the book.

Established in 1966, the Library and Information Technology Association is the division of the American Library Association (ALA) that provides its members and the library and information science community as a whole with a forum for discussion, an environment for learning, and a program for actions on the design, development, and implementation of automated and technological systems in the library and information science field.

Approximately 25 LITA Guides were published by Neal-Schuman and ALA between 2007 and 2015. Rowman & Littlefield took over publication of the series beginning in late 2015. Books in the series published by Rowman & Littlefield are

Digitizing Flat Media: Principles and Practices
The Librarian's Introduction to Programming Languages
Library Service Design: A LITA Guide to Holistic Assessment, Insight, and Improvement
Data Visualization: A Guide to Visual Storytelling for Librarians
Mobile Technologies in Libraries: A LITA Guide
Innovative LibGuides Applications
Integrating LibGuides into Library Websites

Innovative LibGuides Applications

Real-World Examples

Edited by
Ryan L. Sittler
Aaron W. Dobbs

ROWMAN & LITTLEFIELD
Lanham • Boulder • New York • London

Published by Rowman & Littlefield
A wholly owned subsidary of The Rowman & Littlefield Publishing Group, Inc.
4501 Forbes Boulevard, Suite 200, Lanham, Maryland 20706
www.rowman.com

Unit A, Whitacre Mews, 26-34 Stannary Street, London SE11 4AB

Copyright © 2016 by American Library Association

All rights reserved. No part of this book may be reproduced in any form or by any electronic or mechanical means, including information storage and retrieval systems, without written permission from the publisher, except by a reviewer who may quote passages in a review.

British Library Cataloguing in Publication Information Available

Library of Congress Cataloging-in-Publication Data
Names: Sittler, Ryan L., editor. | Dobbs, Aaron W., 1968– editor.
Title: Innovative LibGuides applications : real-world examples / edited by Ryan L. Sittler, Aaron W. Dobbs.
Description: Lanham : Rowman & Littlefield, [2016] | Series: Library Information Technology Association (LITA) guides | Includes bibliographical references and index. | Description based on print version record and CIP data provided by publisher; resource not viewed.
Identifiers: LCCN 2016040542 (print) | LCCN 2016019703 (ebook) | ISBN 9781442270558 (electronic) | ISBN 9781442270534 (cloth : alk. paper) | ISBN 9781442270541 (pbk. : alk. paper)
Subjects: LCSH: LibGuides. | Web applications in libraries.
Classification: LCC Z674.75.W67 (print) | LCC Z674.75.W67 I56 2016 (ebook) | DDC 025.04—dc23 LC record available at https://lccn.loc.gov/2016040542

∞™ The paper used in this publication meets the minimum requirements of American National Standard for Information Sciences—Permanence of Paper for Printed Library Materials, ANSI/NISO Z39.48-1992.

Printed in the United States of America

To our (now retired) Third Amigo: Dr. Douglas Cook.
Thank you for your guidance, humor, and patience. We are eternally grateful.

Contents

Part III. Digital Collections

Part IV. Data-Driven Decision Making

Part V. Information Literacy

Part VI. Library Administration

Part VII. System-Wide Case Study

Figures and Tables

FIGURES

TABLES

Foreword

If you've picked up this book, you're likely hoping to find ways to make the most of your LibGuides subscription. You won't be disappointed.

As budgets shrink and pressure for innovation increases, we are constantly exhorted to "do more with less." For many libraries, this means doing more with LibGuides. As an early adopter of LibGuides and former Springshare employee, I've communicated with hundreds of librarians using LibGuides, and I've observed the ways in which both the community and the vendor have adapted the product to meet the needs of libraries and librarians. Despite the fear that LibGuides is a hammer and everything looks like a nail, many libraries are making truly thoughtful and inventive use of the software.

Within these pages, you'll find inspiration on how LibGuides and other Springshare products can be used to improve your key services (such as reference and instruction), as well as best practices on data collection, accessibility, and using LibGuides as a teaching tool. Since failure is a key part of the innovation process, you'll also find refreshingly frank discussions about what didn't work.

Even LibGuides experts will find something of interest in this book—I know I did!

Laura J. Harris, MSI
Online Learning Librarian
State University of New York, Oswego

Preface

Innovative LibGuides Applications: Real-World Examples was born from our desire to see how colleagues were using LibGuides at their institutions in ways that other folks were not. We received lots of fantastic proposals from a variety of libraries (and countries) and had a difficult time winnowing them down to the fifteen chapters you'll see represented here. Ultimately, we had to pick the chapters that fit together most cohesively and augmented each other—while repeating content as little as possible. We hope you'll be happy with what you find here. The book is broken into seven broad categories: Website Integration, Learning Management System Integration, Digital Collections, Data-Driven Decision Making, Information Literacy, Library Administration, and a System-Wide Case Study.

Our goal in addressing these categories was not to be exhaustive, but instead to give you a broad taste of how people are choosing to use LibGuides/LibApps in ways that have been successful—or not. Likewise, raw building blocks are included in various ways (e.g., code snippets, images, walk-throughs) so that you can build upon and implement these ideas at your own institutions. Naturally, if you have questions about these concepts, you are welcome to contact the original authors for each chapter. Some have chosen to provide contact information—if they have not and you are unable to find them, please contact the editors and we will put you in touch. Likewise, Springshare recently announced a new product called LibWizard that will help with building instructional materials. Unfortunately, at the time of writing, this product is not available. But don't fret; we're looking forward to addressing it at some point in the future!

This book is written for a wide audience. Some chapters are necessarily more technical in nature compared to others. Likewise, some utilize a lot of images while others do not. Nonetheless, we hope that you'll read, enjoy, and get something out of each chapter. If you can find even one new thing to utilize at your institution, we'll be happy. So please, enjoy this book! An overview of each section of this book follows.

WEBSITE INTEGRATION

Some institutions are using LibGuides *as* their library webpage. Others are integrating it and LibApps with a broader website management package such as WordPress or specific software such as EZProxy. This is all due to the fact that LibGuides/ LibApps offers a lot of customizability. This section looks at how four institutions are using the software in very different ways to meet their local needs.

LEARNING MANAGEMENT SYSTEM INTEGRATION

This section examines two very different approaches to learning management systems (LMS)—with one chapter looking at how to integrate functionality with Moodle and the other looking at how LibGuides could be used as its own LMS. The results in both cases are quite interesting and definitely worth reading regardless of whether your institution is planning on going in one of these directions. Even if you are not using Moodle, the concepts addressed in that chapter can apply to most LMS packages.

DIGITAL COLLECTIONS

Some institutions are thinking outside of the box when it comes to LibGuides/ LibApps usage. This section shows two very different approaches to providing access to digital collections on the LibGuides framework. One method involves the design of a digital museum while the other looks at exhibitions and their application as outreach tools. These two dichotomous approaches could, generally speaking, be implemented at any library immediately.

DATA-DRIVEN DECISION MAKING

LibGuides/LibApps creates—and provides—a lot of data for users to mine and utilize in various ways. This section will show you how two different institutions utilized this data in very different ways to improve services in various ways.

INFORMATION LITERACY

Information literacy instruction is always a worthwhile topic to discuss. You will find two approaches that you could utilize to start revamping your instruction program—with LibGuides/LibApps as a key part of that transition. Both face-to-face and distance instruction are addressed.

LIBRARY ADMINISTRATION

Many people think of LibGuides/LibApps in terms of students (in academia) or, in many cases, general patronage. This section looks at both internal and external processes that can be augmented by creative use of the LibGuides platform. Like many other chapters, these are applications that you could implement quickly and easily to improve services.

SYSTEM-WIDE CASE STUDY

The final section of the book is a unique look into how a system of community colleges in North Carolina are each using LibGuides/LibApps, in various ways, to improve and supplement their services. This is a broad-based case study that is systemic as opposed to just being institution-specific. It also includes survey data and direct interview questions from LibGuides users in North Carolina.

You may wish to also look at this book's sister publication, *Integrating LibGuides into Library Websites*, if you want a broader introduction to LibGuides/LibApps and want ideas for administration, maintenance, and broader design.

Acknowledgments

Where do we start? Lots of people played a role in getting this book to press and we're grateful for all of them. I suppose we should start by thanking the folks at Springshare for producing—and continuously improving—the LibGuides and LibApps products. We've both been users for quite a while, and we're both continuously impressed by not only the improvements that are pushed out to users, but also the creative ways in which users find to use them.

Which leads us to the next group that we need to thank: the entire Springshare user community and—particularly—those folks who submitted chapter proposals for the book. It is your collective innovative and forward-thinking ideas that helped produce this book. We couldn't accept every proposal, but they were all valuable in their own way. We only wish we could have included each of them.

Next, we'd like to thank LITA managing editor, Marta Deyrup, and our Rowman & Littlefield editor, Charles Harmon, for helping us throughout this process. Additionally, thank you to Laura Harris for fact-checking and writing our foreword. We also need to recognize our good (retired) friend, Dr. Doug Cook. We did our best to remember all of the guidance he has given us over the years. We also tried to maintain his level of humor (though really, without Doug, it just isn't possible). Finally, Ryan would like to thank his wife, Heatherlee, for her legendary love and patience while he worked to try and hit his deadline. And Aaron would like to thank his wife, Julie, and daughters, Natasha and Alena, and his whole work gang for their generosity, patience, and fortitude as the editorial process ran down to the wire.

1

LibGuides as Library Homepage

Rebuilding the LibGuides Default Template

Jeremy Hall, University of North Florida

Is your organization considering converting your library homepage to the Lib-Guides platform? Do you simply wish to replicate many of the functions and overall user interface of your homepage? Are you simply trying to unify your total web presence with one distinctive style that differs from the default LibGuides template? Are you already using LibGuides to create course and subject guides? In that case, why not unify your web presence into a single system? Does your existing platform adequately meet your needs? Is access and control at a level that you require? Does your information technology department provide strong enough support to your existing web presence?

At the University of North Florida, we made the decision to build out Lib-Guides as a future replacement for our homepage largely due to the shortcomings of the official university content management system (CMS). The university CMS was outdated and completely unable to support dynamic content. The library homepage was little more than a published document rather than a living webpage. Further, changes of any kind were slow to implement and typically could not be made in real time. Finally, the complexity of the university CMS was such that the vast majority of faculty and staff did not have the skill set necessary to use the system. This meant that even the simplest edits could only be performed by a select group of individuals.

There are a variety of excellent reasons why LibGuides version 2 (LGv2) might be a great choice for your institution—it supports dynamic content, updates in real time, and is extremely easy to use without requiring any specialized technical skills. And with a few customizations, it can be adapted to build a unique, effective website. Please note that all the customizations described below can be seen in a live environment at libguides.unf.edu/, at least until we make more changes!

GETTING STARTED WITH CUSTOMIZATION

HTML and CSS

Most customizations in LibGuides will require at least a working knowledge of both Hyper Text Markup Language (HMTL) and Cascading Style Sheets (CSS). HTML is a standardized protocol used to publish documents on the web and is the foundation of most content on the World Wide Web. HTML is used to create content, and CSS is used to describe the presentation of webpages. This includes information about colors, fonts, and layouts.

Bootstrap and the CSS Grid System

LibGuides is largely structured around an excellent open-source CSS framework called Bootstrap (getbootstrap.com/), and learning about it is great for LGv2 customization. Bootstrap 3, at the time of writing, is an open-source framework and the foundation for the structure and organization of LGv2. CSS frameworks are basically libraries of CSS files that can be used to kick start web development. Common elements such as typography, icons, buttons, and layout are predefined so designers can concentrate on creating content. Bootstrap is fully developed, which means that LGv2 can support a comprehensive batch of robust options right out of the box. It is not necessary to master Bootstrap to successfully customize LGv2. However, developing a minimal understanding of Bootstrap, particularly the grid system, will prove immensely helpful as LGv2 comes with all the necessary files to allow you to utilize anything within the Bootstrap framework.

There is a wide variety of existing CSS classes within Bootstrap that may be utilized in LibGuides. These classes cover just about anything you're ever likely to do without having to create the basic CSS from scratch, though you may need to make some minor tweaks. Many of these inherent Bootstrap features are useful and include navigation options, menus, tabs, carousels (fancy slide shows that can include more than just images), buttons, and panels. All of these are explained in great detail at getbootstrap.com/ and are fairly easy to grasp if you have a working knowledge of HTML and CSS. Fortunately, if you are not comfortable with HTML and CSS, there are a variety of free sources where you can quickly learn some basic skills, such as the website for W3C schools, www.w3schools.com/.

You will need to familiarize yourself with the Bootstrap grid system if you wish to make changes to the default homepage. Anything but the most basic layout changes will require alterations to the existing grid. However, utilizing the Bootstrap CSS grid system will allow you to significantly alter the base template layout in a manner that doesn't require writing much custom code. The grid is a pre-defined layout consisting of rows and columns where you can place content. You can build a grid skeleton, much like you would build a table, and simply add various components wherever you choose within the grid. Ideally, you should determine what components (e.g., search box, hours of operation, content slider) you would like to include and then build a grid to accommodate those selections.

The Bootstrap grid system is predefined with twelve equal columns in rows that span the entire width of the browser. These columns are defined via unique CSS classes that tell a Web browser how to display a given element. These columns can be used individually or together in any combination with the .col-md-* class so long as each row equals twelve. There are a variety of grid styles, but the default LibGuides grid uses the stacked to horizontal method. When viewed on a standard size Mac or PC, the browser will display your rows and columns just like a standard table, but on mobile devices the grid will instead "stack" the columns vertically.

Figure 1.1 shows four different options using various pieces of the .col-md-* class including the HTML markup and a visual depiction. These are by no means

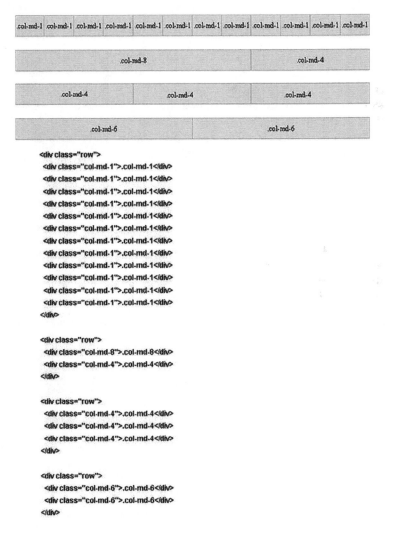

Figure 1.1.   Four examples of the Bootstrap grid with accompanying code.

exclusive as any combination of twelve can be used to create a row with our grid. The first is a row of twelve equal columns that is achieved by stringing the .col-md-1 class twelve times consecutively. Most users probably don't have a good use for a row like this as it basically replicates a table. The second example is a more common two-column layout split between a first column that covers two-thirds (.col-md-8) of the grid row and a second column that fills the remaining one third (.col-md-4). Incidentally, this just so happens to be the structure Springshare chose for the default LibGuides template. The third example is a row divided equally into thirds (.col-md-4). Finally, the last row is an example of dividing a row exactly in half with two equal (.col-md-6) columns.

Modifying the Default Template

The default template provided by Springshare divides the homepage into two unequal columns, exactly as configured in the second row of the example in figure 1.1. The first column is essentially two-thirds of the row (being eight grid columns wide using the .col-md-8 class) with the second column comprising the remaining one-third of the row (being four grid columns utilizing the .col-md-4 class). If you were to strip down the base template to nothing but the Bootstrap grid and remove all the content, the markup would look like figure 1.2.

```
<div class="row">
   <div class="col-md-8">.col-md-8</div>
   <div class="col-md-4">.col-md-4</div>
</div>
```

Figure 1.2.   The Bootstrap grid from the LibGuides template without the excess code.

The template actually includes far more than just the Bootstrap grid. There are many components, but for now, we are only concerned with everything below <!--content!--> as this is where we will find the grid as depicted in figure 1.3.

You may notice some unusual features in this markup. First, each row in the grid has an additional class called .clearfix. While not absolutely necessary, it is strongly advised to use this as the .clearfix class will help alleviate potential column offset issues. Springshare has wisely included .clearfix into their grid and you should too.

Next, you may notice that each of our columns classes has been appended with -center. This is another Bootstrap option than can help improve positioning. Again, while not necessary, this will ensure that the entire row stays centered on the page, even if the width of the body area is wider than the width of your row.

```html
<body class="s-lib-public-body">
    <!-- BEGIN: Page Header -->
    {{public_header}}
    <!-- END: Page Header -->
    <!-- BEGIN: Content Header -->
    <div id="s-lib-public-header" class="s-lib-header container s-lib-side-borders">
        <div id="s-lib-bc">
            {{breadcrumbs}}
        </div>
        <h1 id="s-lib-public-header-title">{{title}}
</h1>
        <div id="s-lib-public-header-desc">{{system_intro}}
</div>
    </div>
    <!-- END: Content Header -->
    <!-- BEGIN: Nav Bar -->
    <div id="s-lib-public-nav" class="container s-lib-side-borders">
        {{page_nav}}
    </div>
    <!-- END: Nav Bar -->
    <!-- BEGIN: content -->
    <div id="s-lib-public-main" class="s-lib-main container s-lib-side-borders">
        <div id="s-lg-index-cols" class="row">
            <div id="col1" class="col-md-8 center">
                <div class="clearfix">
                    <div id="s-lg-hp-nav">
                        <ul>
                            <li>
                                <ul class="nav nav-pills">
                                    {{button_all_guides}}
                                    {{button_by_group}}
                                    {{button_by_subject}}
                                    {{button_by_type}}
                                    {{button_by_owner}}
                                </ul>
                            <li>
                            <li id="s-lg-hp-nav-bottom">
                                <div class="clearfix">
                                    {{search_guides}}
                                </div>
                            </li>
                        </ul>
                    </div>
                    {{guide_list_controls}}
                </div>
                <div id="s-lg-index-list" class="">
                    {{content}}
                </div>
            </div>
            <div id="col2" class="col-md-4 center">
                {{content_boxes}}
            </div>
        </div>
    </div>
    <!-- END: content -->
    <!-- BEGIN: Page Footer -->
    {{system_footer}}
    <!-- END: Page Footer -->
    <div id="s-lib-alert" title="">
        <div id="s-lib-alert-content"></div>
    </div>
    <div id="s-lib-popover-title" class="hide">
        <span class="text-info"><strong>title</strong></span>
        <button type="button" id="popclose" class="close" onclick="jQuery('.s-lib-popover').popover('hide')">&times;</button>
    </div>
    <div id="s-lib-popover-content" class="hide"><i class="fa fa-refresh fa-spin"></i> Loading...
        <button class="btn btn-default btn-sm popclose" type="button">Close</button>
    </div>
    <div id="s-lib-scroll-top" title="Back to Top">
        <span class="fa-stack fa-lg">
            <i class="fa fa-square-o fa-stack-2x"></i>
            <i class="fa fa-angle-double-up fa-stack-1x" style="position:relative; bottom:2px;"></i>
        </span>
    </div>     <!-- BEGIN: Custom Footer -->
    {{public_footer}}
    <!-- END: Custom Footer -->
</body>
```

Figure 1.3.   The complete Springshare template.

If you choose, as discussed later in this chapter, you may keep this default grid structure and simply swap out or add new components and keywords. This is the easiest way to alter the default content. On the other hand, if you would prefer a completely different style layout, you may do away with this altogether and build your own grid from scratch. I'm going to utilize the default structure but add an additional full-width row to create a different layout as seen in figure 1.4. The markup for this grid is displayed in figure 1.5.

Our grid consists of two distinct rows instead of the single-row structure of the default template. The first row is really nothing more than the same structure as the default LGv2 grid but with significantly altered content. The standard LibGuides search box and all content located in .col-md-8 center has been completely removed and replaced by a content slider and a discovery tool search box. The content that was located in .col-md-4 center has also been removed and replaced by custom widgets for LibCal and LibAnswers. I've also added a second brand new row consisting of one single column where the standard LibGuides search box has been relocated. This is our new grid structure.

Figure 1.4.   **LGv2 homepage example.**

```
<div class="row">
  <div id="col1" class="col-md-8 center">
   <div class="clearfix">
    Insert 1st Column Content
   </div>
  </div>
  <div id="col2" class="col-md-4 center">
   <div class="clearfix">
    Insert 2nd Column Content
   </div>
  </div>
</div>
<div class="row">
  <div id="col1" class="col-md-12 center">
   <div class="clearfix">
    Insert Content
   </div>
  </div>
</div>
```

Figure 1.5. The markup for figure 1.4.

As you examine the default template we started with, you will also note that there are some strange items, marked inside of curly brackets {{}}, scattered throughout the markup. These curly-bracketed items are referred to by Springshare as "keywords" and are markers for precoded snippets that can be placed anywhere in the markup. Place the keyword someplace in the grid and the code will execute as if it were written in that location. In our grid example, we simply copied the entire existing markup for the LibGuides search box and pasted it into our new single-column row.

For a simple example of how this works, we will work with the {{breadcrumbs}} keyword. Springshare has defined the {{breadcrumbs}} keyword so that it will output navigational breadcrumbs as: *System Name>Group Name>Guide Name>Page Name*. The default template places {{breadcrumbs}} near the top of the content header just before the {{title}} keyword as seen in figure 1.6.

This is a fairly typical location to place breadcrumbs and probably a good one. When viewed, the actual page would display the breadcrumbs across the top of the content section of the page, just above the welcome message (keyword {{title}}) and introductory text (keyword {{system_intro}}) as in figure 1.7.

This looks nice, but what if you wanted to move it somewhere else? Easy! All we need to do is remove {{breadcrumbs}} from the markup and move it to the new location. We are going to move the breadcrumbs to a position below the welcome message and introductory text in the next example. The new markup is in figure 1.8. Just like that, our breadcrumbs are now in a new position as seen in figure 1.9.

```
<!-- BEGIN: Content Header -->

   <div id="s-lib-public-header" class="s-lib-header container s-lib-side-borders">

      <div id="s-lib-bc">

      {{breadcrumbs}}

      </div>


      <h1 id="s-lib-public-header-title">{{title}}</h1>

      <div id="s-lib-public-header-desc">{{system_intro}}</div>

   </div>

<!-- END: Content Header -->
```

Figure 1.6. The default LibGuides template header markup.

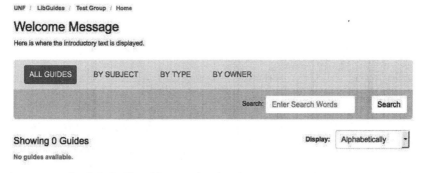

Figure 1.7. The default LibGuides template header.

That's it! It's as simple as cutting and pasting the code to a new location. Springshare provides comprehensive information about the various keywords that are available for use within LibGuides in their help section, and it is worth reading. Again, these keywords can be placed anywhere in your homepage and in individual guide's templates. Once you've decided on your grid, it's a matter of copying and pasting code or inserting keywords in the proper locations.

Building a Header

If you choose, you could just simply upload an image file to the header and avoid code entirely. This is a perfectly acceptable method of creating a header, but

```
<!-- BEGIN: Content Header -->

    <div id="s-lib-public-header" class="s-lib-header container s-lib-side-borders">


        <h1 id="s-lib-public-header-title">{{title}}</h1>

        <div id="s-lib-public-header-desc">{{system_intro}}</div>


    <div id="s-lib-bc">

        {{breadcrumbs}}

    </div>

    </div>

    <!-- END: Content Header -->
```

Figure 1.8. The {{breadcrumbs}} keyword has been relocated in the markup.

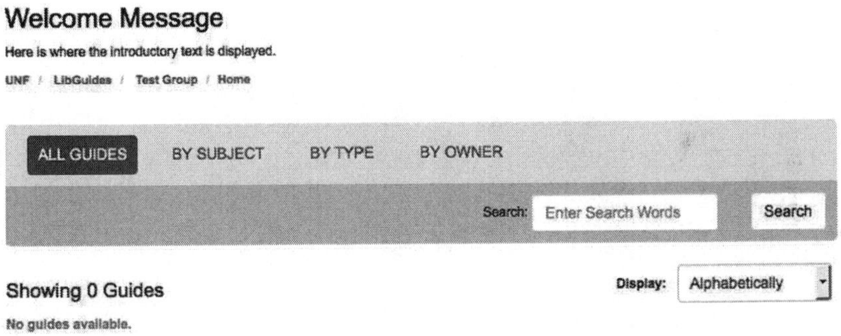

Welcome Message
Here is where the introductory text is displayed.

UNF / LibGuides / Test Group / Home

| ALL GUIDES | BY SUBJECT | BY TYPE | BY OWNER |

Search: [Enter Search Words] [Search]

Showing 0 Guides   Display: [Alphabetically ▾]

No guides available.

Figure 1.9.   Browser view of the relocated {{breadcrumbs}} keyword.

it does present some problems if you need something more elaborate. The custom header field in LibGuides is no different than the custom template. All of the same options are available. What does this mean? You may build a grid in your header and place content just like you would in the body. Use this link to view an example: libguides.unf.edu/.

This header is built using the same Bootstrap grid used in the default template body: two columns of differing width using first the .col-md-8 class and then the .col-md-4 class. A few images were added, as well as a search box, to complete the main header. Placing your code in the header is simple: visit the LibGuides Admin module and navigate to Look & Feel then to Header/Footer/Tabs/Boxes tab in the Admin Panel under Page Header. Now there is one final touch—how about adding fully functional drop-down navigation?

Adding a Menu

Sure, you have a beautiful LibGuides search box, which can be used to find any of your guides, but what if you would like to have an actual menu? Fortunately, Bootstrap has a mobile-friendly default navigation (navbar) that you can use to serve as a primary menu for your new LibGuides homepage. This packaged navbar can easily be added to LibGuides, right below the grid you built inside your custom header, by placing the markup directly after your grid. The basic Bootstrap markup you'll need to start with looks like figure 1.10.

```
<nav class="navbar navbar-default">
  <div class="container-fluid">
    <!-- Brand and toggle get grouped for better mobile display -->
    <div class="navbar-header">
      <button type="button" class="navbar-toggle collapsed" data-toggle="collapse" data-target="#bs-example-navbar-collapse-1" aria-expanded="false">
        <span class="sr-only">Toggle navigation</span>
        <span class="icon-bar"></span>
        <span class="icon-bar"></span>
        <span class="icon-bar"></span>
      </button>
      <a class="navbar-brand" href="#">Brand</a>
    </div>

    <!-- Collect the nav links, forms, and other content for toggling -->
    <div class="collapse navbar-collapse" id="bs-example-navbar-collapse-1">
      <ul class="nav navbar-nav">
        <li class="active"><a href="#">Link <span class="sr-only">(current)</span></a></li>
        <li><a href="#">Link</a></li>
        <li class="dropdown">
          <a href="#" class="dropdown-toggle" data-toggle="dropdown" role="button" aria-haspopup="true" aria-expanded="false">Dropdown <span class="caret"></span></a>
          <ul class="dropdown-menu">
            <li><a href="#">Action</a></li>
            <li><a href="#">Another action</a></li>
            <li><a href="#">Something else here</a></li>
            <li role="separator" class="divider"></li>
            <li><a href="#">Separated link</a></li>
            <li role="separator" class="divider"></li>
            <li><a href="#">One more separated link</a></li>
          </ul>
        </li>
      </ul>
      <form class="navbar-form navbar-left" role="search">
        <div class="form-group">
          <input type="text" class="form-control" placeholder="Search">
        </div>
        <button type="submit" class="btn btn-default">Submit</button>
      </form>
      <ul class="nav navbar-nav navbar-right">
        <li><a href="#">Link</a></li>
        <li class="dropdown">
          <a href="#" class="dropdown-toggle" data-toggle="dropdown" role="button" aria-haspopup="true" aria-expanded="false">Dropdown <span class="caret"></span></a>
          <ul class="dropdown-menu">
            <li><a href="#">Action</a></li>
            <li><a href="#">Another action</a></li>
            <li><a href="#">Something else here</a></li>
            <li role="separator" class="divider"></li>
            <li><a href="#">Separated link</a></li>
          </ul>
        </li>
      </ul>
    </div><!-- /.navbar-collapse -->
  </div><!-- /.container-fluid -->
</nav>
```

Figure 1.10. Markup for the Bootstrap menu.

This default navbar will require some additional customization to suit your needs. Load it and take a look so you can see how the various options actually work. You may find that you do not need all of the assigned classes, so remove any that are unnecessary and add your links. The only styling you will have at first is the Bootstrap default. Next, you will want to style your menu with CSS to match your color scheme and design. This may require some experimentation, as a wide variety of classes may need to be altered. Not mentioned in the Bootstrap documentation: by default the menus are only drop-down on click. However, it is possible to add a drop-down on mouse-over effect with just a single line of CSS as shown in figure 1.11.

```
.dropdown:hover .dropdown-menu {

display:block;

}
```

Figure 1.11.   This CSS will transform your Bootstrap menu into a drop-down menu.

SPRINGSHARE WIDGET INTEGRATION AND OTHER CUSTOMIZATIONS

Widgets provide a way for you to integrate functions or features of other applications, in this case referring to other Springshare products, directly into your custom LGv2 instance. You may have a LibAnswers 2 subscription at your institution—why force your users to visit LibAnswers directly when asking a question? You can use tools within LibAnswers to build an embeddable "ask a question" widget that can be dropped directly into your LibGuides homepage. Using widgets gives your users access to more tools without having to visit multiple pages. The options are limitless as Springshare is providing almost total access to their LGv2 templates, as well as robust widget builders, in each of their software packages. The following are a few common tools that most folks will probably wish to use, regardless of how you are using LGv2.

Discovery Tool

What's a library homepage without the ability to search materials? Fortunately, most vendors provide access to an application program interface (API) or a search box builder. An API is nothing more than a kind of software intermediary that makes it possible for seemingly unrelated programs to integrate or share date with each other. Typically, you do not need to have a deep understanding of the code involved. You simply follow some basic instructions from your vendor and the API will provide you with the necessary code. All you really need to do at that point is copy and paste the code into whichever grid space you would like your search box to appear.

Springshare Widgets

If you happen to subscribe to other Springshare products, such as LibCal or LibAnswers, then you are in luck! LibCal is a web-based calendar solution that includes the ability to manage room bookings, event calendars, and appointments. LibAnswers is an all-in-one reference platform that includes live chat, FAQs, Short Message Service (SMS), and social media integration. All of these Springshare products come packaged with a robust API and the ability to create a wide variety of easy-to-use widgets. Inserting widgets into LibGuides is as simple as copying the code and pasting it directly into your grid. Please note that if you are still using version 1 of LibAnswers or LibCal, most widgets will function poorly or sometimes not at all.

Carousel

The customization that I am most often asked about is how to add a carousel or slider. A carousel or slider is just a fancy slideshow that can include not only images but also HTML, widgets, or anything you would like to rotate. Once again, Bootstrap is the easy answer. Bootstrap comes packaged with a JavaScript carousel all ready to go. You just need to insert the code and then style with CSS as shown in figure 1.12.

```html
<div id="carousel-example-generic" class="carousel slide" data-ride="carousel">

  <!-- Indicators -->

  <ol class="carousel-indicators">
    <li data-target="#carousel-example-generic" data-slide-to="0" class="active"></li>
    <li data-target="#carousel-example-generic" data-slide-to="1"></li>
    <li data-target="#carousel-example-generic" data-slide-to="2"></li>
  </ol>

  <!-- Wrapper for slides -->

  <div class="carousel-inner" role="listbox">
    <div class="item active">
      <img src="..." alt="...">
      <div class="carousel-caption">
        ...
      </div>
    </div>
    <div class="item">
      <img src="..." alt="...">
      <div class="carousel-caption">
        ...
      </div>
    </div>
    ...
  </div>

  <!-- Controls -->

  <a class="left carousel-control" href="#carousel-example-generic" role="button" data-slide="prev">
    <span class="glyphicon glyphicon-chevron-left" aria-hidden="true"></span>
    <span class="sr-only">Previous</span>
  </a>
  <a class="right carousel-control" href="#carousel-example-generic" role="button" data-slide="next">
    <span class="glyphicon glyphicon-chevron-right" aria-hidden="true"></span>
    <span class="sr-only">Next</span>
  </a>
</div>
```

Figure 1.12.   Markup for the Bootstrap carousel.

CONCLUSION

Ideally, the information provided here will serve as a nice starting point to build your own unique LibGuides homepage, but I hope it's not the endpoint! Experiment. Do not be afraid to try something new. LGv2 CMS comes with the ability to create multiple "groups"—under "Admin" select "Groups" to create a new group—which can each have their own unique homepage utilizing the exact same templates as the default LGv2 homepage. What this means is that you can create a sandbox group that is hidden from the public where you can try out different templates, different configurations, or new widgets. You can also make any group private so that your users don't stumble upon it. This allows you to test anything before you add it to your live page.

LibGuides shouldn't be a static page that you simply build and walk away from. Rather, it should be an organic tool that grows and changes to benefit your staff, students, and faculty. At the University of North Florida, we have pursued a layered approach. There is dynamic content that updates in real time, such as our Twitter feed. Likewise, some content updates daily, such as hours of operation and our events calendar. Other content updates less frequently. We may add/remove content from our carousel on a daily/weekly/monthly basis depending upon current marketing of the library needs or to focus on blog articles, special events, or new and improved services. This is where dynamic widgets can really be your friend; you achieve constant updates without having to make manual changes.

There is no one-size-fits-all plan, nor is there a perfect LibGuides configuration. The needs of your institution may not be the same as mine. Your needs today may not necessarily be the needs tomorrow. Conduct a thorough review of your homepage a couple of times a year and address any changing needs. Finally, keep it fresh, keep it relevant, and keep on pushing the envelope. You'll have a fantastically unique version of LGv2 in no time!

2

Incorporating LibAnswers, LibCal, and LibGuides into a WordPress Library Website

Christa E. Poparad, MSLIS, College of Charleston
Angela R. Flenner, MLIS, MSHP, College of Charleston

The new LibApps products from Springshare facilitate the integration of librarian-created content into library websites to a much greater degree than was previously possible. At College of Charleston Libraries, we have taken advantage of this benefit as we've redesigned our own library website. Formerly, the college's content management system (CMS) allowed only designated library personnel to edit specific areas of the site. Therefore, editable content had to be routed through identified systems librarians with web-coding skills. If a database needed to be added, an event promoted, or a service advertised, the proposed website updates needed to be requested, discussed, and approved before any changes could be made. In addition, some areas of the website were managed by departments outside the library and were not available for editing at all. This constrained the usability of our site as it could not change fast enough to keep pace with the growing array of library resources and services.

In addition to keeping the content fresh, issues such as improving access for our diverse user community across various platforms, streamlining site maintenance, and leveraging library marketing and social media opportunities contributed to the decision to redesign our library website. We wanted it to be more customizable, flexible, and adaptable to users' needs. We also wanted our resources to be device-agnostic—meaning they would translate equally well to smartphones, tablets, and the biggest desktop monitors. We wanted to be able to distribute site maintenance and content creation across library departments as well as to be able to use the virtual real estate provided by our website to promote library resources, services, and events. All of these desires influenced the choices we made during the redesign process.

Looking for sites that aligned with our aspirations helped to inspire us. The websites at Stanford University (library.stanford.edu/), Pennsylvania State University (www.libraries.psu.edu/), and Kent State University (www.library.kent.edu/) all looked more contemporary and addressed the needs of various user communities more effectively than our website. Although we did not want to change the look and feel radically, which would have resulted in an outcry from our users, we did want to improve the functionality of using our site to access library resources and services. Ultimately, we wanted users to be able to find what they needed, using any devices they chose, on a site that was maintained and updated more efficiently.

Our recently relaunched College of Charleston Libraries website (library.cofc. edu/) seamlessly incorporates LibAnswers, LibCal, and LibGuides into the structure of a WordPress site. This addressed our previous website's issues and helped facilitate the ability of librarians and library staff to both maintain current content and add new items expeditiously. WordPress is a platform that began as a simple method to set up a blog but has grown into a fully functional CMS. It is free and open-source, meaning users are able to edit the software as they wish. In addition, its plugin-based system means that other users in the WordPress community can share code that adds features to their sites, and we can download and install these features to ours. The community is large and active, so plugins are available for almost any feature we might think of adding.

To achieve consistency across the WordPress site and LibApps pages, the same Cascading Style Sheet (CSS) is used across both platforms to integrate the page to page transitions as users navigate the site. In addition, the language in LibApps has been customized to blend with terminology used at our institution. Furthermore, both the WordPress site and LibApps are configured in compliance with the College of Charleston Brand Manual (marcomm.cofc.edu/brandmanual/). This is a necessity for a sanctioned site at our institution as it designates colors, fonts, logos, headers, and footers as shown in figure 2.1.

Figure 2.1.   College of Charleston Libraries homepage. *Used by permission of College of Charleston Libraries*

It was important to us that our website content format correctly, across a wide variety of devices, in order to facilitate effective user access to our resources and services. Both the WordPress content and the LibApps content display equally well on mobile and desktop screens. Additionally, both LibApps and our Word-Press site use the Bootstrap framework, which is modular and designed with mobile display in mind. As a result, the pages adjust dynamically based on the user's screen width. Our most recent usage analytics show that around 10 percent of our overall website users are accessing our content on mobile devices, but for certain pages, like LibCal study room reservations, nearly 50 percent of the traffic originates from mobile devices.

SITE DESIGN

Although it is possible to create an entire library website using Springshare products, creating the site using WordPress allows greater flexibility and sophistication for institutions with systems librarians versed in website coding and design. For example, the latest library news is posted on our WordPress site and is syndicated using the Jetpack plugin (wordpress.org/plugins/jetpack/) to our Twitter and Facebook pages. WordPress also allows for a password-protected library staff portal where internal forms, policies, and reports can be posted. Though the WordPress site is maintained by the Digital Scholarship and Services Department, which houses our systems librarians, the integration of Springshare products throughout the site allows librarians and library staff from other departments to maintain their own content—in real time—without the need for extensive coding knowledge.

The website redesign was motivated by a desire to move the library site off the college's campus-wide CMS so that we could provide more timely, flexible, and responsive content to our users. The college's marketing department required us to continue using the college website's header and to conform to the College of Charleston Brand Manual. For this reason, the WordPress-run homepage, all of our LibGuides, and other Springshare LibApps incorporate the college's CSS. We simply refer to our institution's CSS as an external style sheet in the Look & Feel section of LibApps Admin and then troubleshoot any style disagreements between the CSS file and the Libapps HTML code (www.w3schools.com/css/css_howto.asp).

CSS gives priority to whichever piece is called last, so we refer to the college's stylesheets first and then follow that with individual instructions to fix any issues. For example, in LibAnswers, the Browse drop-down bar at the top of the page was misaligned when first applied to our stylesheet. Adding additional lines of CSS regarding the .navbar padding and margin sizes allowed us to override the existing stylesheet and realign the Browse bar options as shown in figure 2.2.

LibAnswers browse bar before CSS edits

LibAnswers browse bar, after addition of the following code to Custom JS/CSS field in LibAnswers Admin:
.navbar .nav>li>a {padding: 16px 15px;}

Figure 2.2.   LibAnswers browse bar before and after CSS edits. *Used by permission of College of Charleston Libraries*

Homepage Tabs and Flyout Menus

Tabs are a main feature of the library homepage, and they offer entry to five major areas of the library's resources. The tabs are labeled: Discover, Ask Us, E-Journals, Databases, and Guides. All but the Discover and E-Journals tabs include LibApps widgets or search boxes. Our colleague, digital services librarian Tyler Mobley, implemented the tabs using the WordPress plugin Tabby Responsive Tabs (wordpress.org/plugins/tabby-responsive-tabs/). The tabs are customizable using CSS and display well on mobile devices.

We originally planned to have a horizontal bar at the top of the page for the main navigation links. However, in order to conform to college website standards (marcomm.cofc.edu/brandmanual/bychapter/webeleccomm/wc_genwebstandards.php), we had to use the college-wide navigation banner. This includes a horizontal navigation bar with institutional links. We changed to a vertical menu in the left column in order to differentiate library links from institutional links. Flyout menus are used to facilitate library site navigation, which includes three broad categories: About, Services, and Research. These menus appear as a user hovers over the category, which simplifies the look of the main page but allows for a large number of pages to be directly linked from the homepage. Our digital services librarian created these flyout menus with UberMenu (wpmegamenu.com/), a WordPress plugin that is very customizable in both style and functionality. Links to various LibApps are included in the menus that lead users to the information they seek.

LibAnswers—Ask Us

Research and Instruction Services maintains LibAnswers. We've branded this service as "Ask Us." The Ask Us tab on the library homepage integrates LibAnswers (answers.library.cofc.edu/) into the site and encourages users to chat live with our Information Desk staff. It also allows users to search our knowledgebase for answers to their questions. The tab includes two LibApps widgets—a LibChat popout button and LibAnswers embedded Search Form Widget. We used the LibApps Custom CSS option to incorporate our college colors into the widget and to better integrate the button and search box into our site. The tab also includes the Information Desk's phone number, text number, and e-mail address for users who prefer those methods of contact. In addition, the "How Do I . . . ?" links on the Services and Research flyout menus lead to the main LibAnswers page.

LibCal—Study Room Reservations and Library Hours

Circulation Services maintains self-service study room bookings in LibCal. Study rooms (libcal.library.cofc.edu/booking/study/) may be reserved from the Services flyout menu of the website as depicted in figure 2.3. Our study room policy (library. cofc.edu/study-room-policy/) is designed so that the students can reserve and police the rooms themselves without library staff involvement. Reserving one of our twenty study rooms requires a student to choose a room and time slot in LibCal and then enter a name and College of Charleston e-mail address. The student must confirm a reservation within thirty minutes by clicking the link sent to his or her e-mail account. The time slots are one hour long, and a student may reserve up to two hours per day. We found that confirmation e-mails were likely to get caught in the students' spam filters until we set an on-campus "From" e-mail account rather than the default Springshare account. In LibCal, this can be set from *Admin>System Settings>Email Settings*. The e-mails now come from the library's Circulation Desk e-mail account.

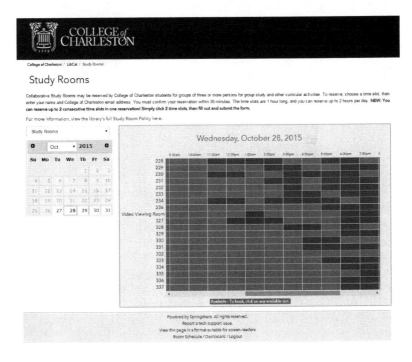

Figure 2.3.   Study rooms. *Used by permission of College of Charleston Libraries*

Links to the libraries' hours (library.cofc.edu/about/hours-3/), also maintained in LibCal, are available on the main webpage under Quick Info and in the About flyout menu. Addlestone Library, the main campus library, is listed first and followed by the main service desks and the branch libraries. Using LibCal's Hours module under Admin, as shown in figure 2.4, our associate dean for public services created the templates for the library's standard weekly opening hours. This includes exceptions for holidays, such as being closed or having shorter hours, and exam times. During exams we are open twenty-four hours per day.

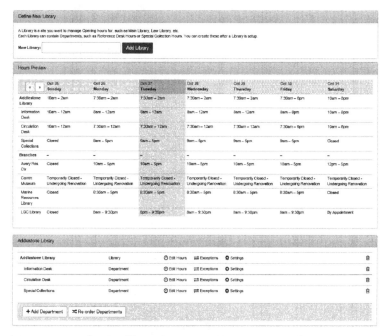

Figure 2.4. Configuring library hours. *Used by permission of Springshare, LLC*

In addition, under the Widgets tab in the Hours module, a JavaScript widget for today's hours can be created and embedded in various LibGuides used throughout the site (e.g., libguides.library.cofc.edu/infodesk). In these instances, we wanted the library hours to be centered in particular boxes. The widget-generated code is aligned to the left by default and cannot be adjusted within the generator itself. Therefore, we added align="center" inside the <div> element of the generated code to specify the centered horizontal alignment of the content. You can see this in figure 2.5.

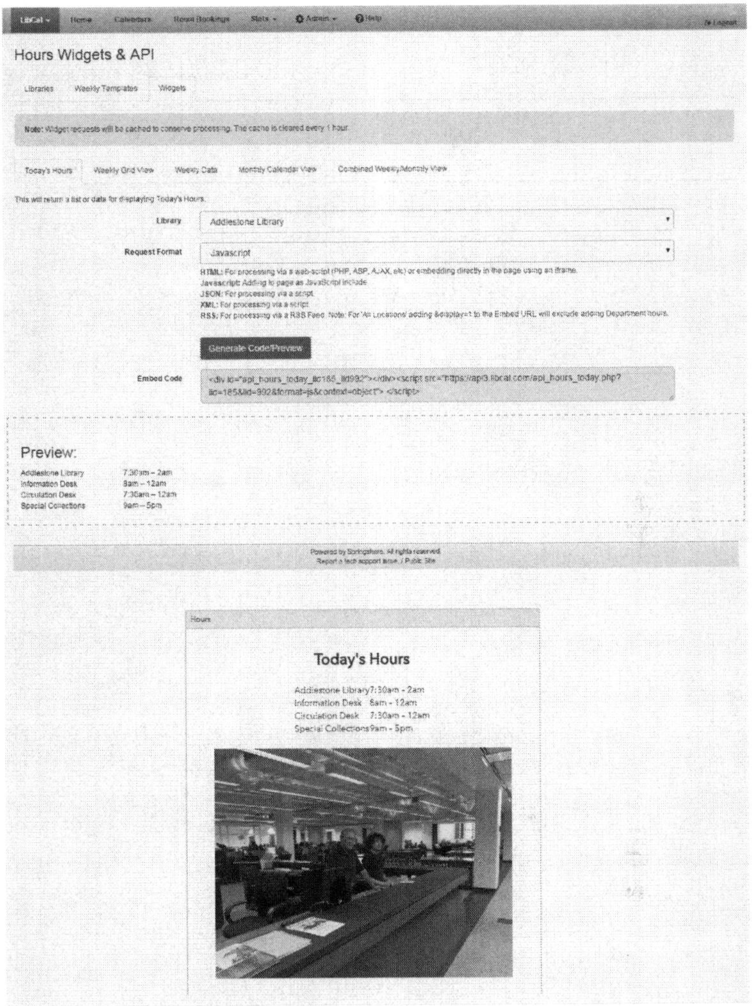

Figure 2.5.   Configuring library hours widget and display in LibGuides. *Used by permission of Springshare, LLC*

LibGuides

LibGuides comprise major portions of the library website. This allows individual library departments to update their content quickly and easily. We customized LibGuides heavily to match the look and feel of our website and to lead our users to essential content. In some cases, code was added to specific templates accessed at *Admin>Look & Feel>Page Layout*, while in other cases, wording was changed in specific system labels (denoted by Key Id) accessed at *Admin>Look & Feel>Language Options>Language Customization*. The complete path is given for each following customization example in order to enable readers to modify their own systems.

LibGuides A–Z Databases

On the A–Z Databases page (libguides.library.cofc.edu/az.php), the full functionality of LibGuides v.2 (LGv2) is employed. This includes search capability for resource title and description, subject associations, vendor drop-down menu, and the ability to highlight new and trial resources. We've also added links to our Journal/Database Request form and our Trial Database Evaluation form. We found that the Language Customization accepted HTML, but the field is limited to 250 characters. For that reason, we needed to use shortened URLs using bit.ly in order to fit in all the text, links, and HTML code we wanted. The path to edit this field from LibGuides Admin is *Look & Feel>Language Options>Language Customization>A-Z Database List>Key Id 40*. We replaced the default text with that in figure 2.6.

```
These databases are newly acquired or
being evaluated for future subscription.
Tell us what you think! <p><ul><li><a
href="http://bit.ly/1f6XHHe">Trial Data-
base Evaluation </a></li><li><a
href="http://bit.ly/1cQdTen">Journal/Dat
abase Request</a></ul></p>
```

Figure 2.6. Custom value for description at the top of the New & Trial Databases section of the A–Z Databases page. *Used by permission of College of Charleston Libraries*

A link to the A–Z Databases page appears on the Research flyout menu. In addition, the Databases tab contains a LibGuides Search Box widget that allows users to search the titles and descriptions of all the databases. It can be found at *Tools>Widgets>Search Box>Search Type>A-Z Databases*. Furthermore, using the alphabet links available on the A–Z Databases page (e.g., libguides.library.cofc.edu/az.php?a=a), we created links on the Databases website tab that start with each letter of the alphabet. Each tab acts as a portal for browsing the list. Digital Scholarship and Services exports data from Serials Solutions to update the list on a periodic basis, Technical Services adds trials and new databases to the list, and Research and Instruction Services updates the database descriptions and subject assignments and reports access issues. This helps to distribute the maintenance workload.

Subject and Course LibGuides

The Guides tab on the main website provides the ability to search or browse subject and course LibGuides. These are branded as Research Guides. The LibGuides widget in this tab is also a Search Box widget that has the Search Type of Guides. It can be found at *Tools>Widgets>Search Box>Search Type>Guides*. Just above the search box in the Guides tab, the header says "Search Research Guides," so we changed the search box placeholder text to say "By Subject or Course Number." A link to the main LibGuides page (libguides.library.cofc.edu/) on the tab and on the Research flyout menu allows users to find guides by subject, type, or librarian. Customizations on this page, found at *Admin>Look & Feel>Language Options>Language Customization>Homepage*, included changing "BY OWNER" to "BY LIBRARIAN" (Key Id 5) and changing "Subject Experts" to "Subject Liaison(s)" (Key Id 27).

We invested a lot of time assigning subjects to the databases in the A-Z List and designating subject homepages, experts, and guides in the Subjects, Tags & URLs module under Admin in order to align resources with our library liaison program. Subject associations are maintained by one of our evening and weekend librarians while individual subject and course guides are maintained by the responsible library liaison.

Furthermore, we customized our subject landing page (libguides.library.cofc.edu/sb.php) and individual subject pages (e.g., libguides.library.cofc.edu/subject_business) by rearranging the content boxes in the right-hand column of our layout. We asked Springshare for their assistance in creating new templates in order to link to the A-Z Database list and LibAnswers, as well as moving the subject experts—renamed subject liaisons—to the top of the column on both the subject landing page and the individual subject homepages. This arrangement emphasizes the liaison librarian as the main point of contact for subject-specific inquiries and complements our recently reorganized library liaison program.

The default template for the individual subject pages under *Admin>Look & Feel>Page Layout>Subject* has content boxes only for Search and Subject Expert and uses page-specific tokens to display these boxes. The relevant code from the default template is in figure 2.7.

```
<div id="col2" class="col-md-4 center">
          <div style="padding-top: 9px;"></div>
          {{content_box_search}}
          {{content_box_experts}}
</div>
```

Figure 2.7. Sidebar text in the default template for sb.php. *Used by permission of Springshare, LLC*

Since tokens like "content_box_search" only work on certain pages, the Springshare support technician created the A-Z Database List link and LibAnswers link using HTML. The relevant code from our customized template, found under *Admin>Look & Feel>Page Layout>Subject*, is in figure 2.8.

We replicated these changes in the subject landing page found under the *Admin>Look & Feel>Page Layout>Subject>Landing Page* tab. In addition, the subject landing page (libguides.library.cofc.edu/sb.php) was retitled Liaisons, Research Guides, and Databases under *Admin>Look & Feel>Language Options>Language*

```
<div  id="col2"  class="col-md-4 center">
      <div style="padding-top: 9px;"></div>
      {{content_box_experts}}

      <div class="margin-bottom-xlg">
          <div class="s-lib-public-side-header">
              <div class="pad-bottom-sm">Need help? Ask Us!
              </div>
          </div>
          <div class="txt pad-top-sm">Chat directly with the Information Desk staff, schedule
a research consultation,   or search our knowledge base.
          </div><a href="http://answers.library.cofc.edu" class="btn btn-info
s-lg-hp-btn-section">Ask Us!</a>
      </div>

      <div class="margin-bottom-xlg">
          <div class="s-lib-public-side-header">
              <div class="pad-bottom-sm">A-Z Database List
              </div>
          </div>
          <div class="txt pad-top-sm">Full list of databases, including trial access.
          </div><a href="/az.php" class="btn btn-info s-lg-hp-btn-section">Go to A-Z
List</a>
      </div>

      {{content_box_search}}

</div>
```

Figure 2.8.   Sidebar text in our customized sb.php page, including links to our A–Z Database List and LibAnswers. *Used by permission of Springshare, LLC*

Customization>Subjects>Key Id 79. On our website, this page is accessed from the Browse Resources by Subject link on the Guides tab and from the Resources by Subject and Subject Liaisons links on the Research flyout menu. The Liaisons, Research Guides, and Databases page provides users with a drop-down menu leading to uniform presentations of subject-associated research guides, databases, and library liaison profiles. "Subject Experts" on the individual subject homepages was changed to "Subject Liaisons" using *Admin>Look & Feel>Language Options>Language Customization>Global>Key Id 45.*

Services and Research LibGuides

Although LibGuides were originally intended as subject and course guides for library resources, we now use them additionally as portals to library services, information literacy instruction, and virtual displays. Many of these guides are linked in the Services and Research flyout menus on the library website. The guides are maintained by the responsible library departments, allowing those with the most knowledge in these areas to update this content efficiently and effectively. Examples include the following:

- Borrow, Renew, Return—Circulation Services (libguides.library.cofc.edu/Circulationservices/Studentborrowing);
- Collection Development—Technical Services (libguides.library.cofc.edu/colldev);
- Digital Scholarship Projects—Digital Scholarship and Services (libguides.library.cofc.edu/dh);

- Undergraduate Student Services—Research and Instruction Services (libguides. library.cofc.edu/undergraduatestudentservices).

CONCLUSION

We redesigned our website with a number of goals that included providing users with a sophisticated portal to the libraries' resources and services while giving librarians and staff control over their own content. We also wanted to achieve this without the need for extensive coding skills. Incorporating both LibGuides and WordPress allowed us to take advantage of both systems. Librarians and staff with little or no coding skills can add their content through LibGuides while those with more advanced coding skills can take advantage of the more powerful WordPress features. Although sections of the College of Charleston Libraries website are maintained by different departments using LibAnswers, LibCal, and LibGuides, employing the same CSS provides a uniform appearance as users navigate across different areas of the site. This marriage of LibApps with WordPress has enabled us to present information to our wide variety of users more directly, in real time, and on any device.

3

Enhancing LibGuides' Usability and Discoverability within a Complex Library Presence

Lisa Campbell, University of Michigan
Ken Varnum, University of Michigan
Albert Bertram, University of Michigan

At the University of Michigan Library, we use LibGuides to manage subject, course, and specialized information guides comprising thousands of individual web pages. While LibGuides can be used to build a robust library website, complete with features for managing electronic reserves and databases, we maintain it as a supplementary tool focused around instruction and guidance. It is one of several open-source and proprietary components making up our library's complex web presence. Our main website (www.lib.umich.edu) is based on the open-source Drupal content management system. We have a multitiered set of discovery interfaces, including a homegrown "bento-box"-style search interface that presents results from multiple sources in a single display. These include the catalog, our Summon-based article discovery service, and our journal and database finder, among others. Our main library catalog interface is powered by the open-source VuFind discovery software that provides a faceted interface to bibliographic records.

It can be challenging to make LibGuides content discoverable and to present it as a functional, integral part of the whole in such a complex online environment. Doing so, however, is critical if we are to efficiently connect users to relevant information resources. In the following chapter, we will share examples of how we have integrated LibGuides into our library website and learning management systems (LMS) in order to facilitate access to content through search and discovery.

HISTORY AND BACKGROUND

When we adopted LibGuides in February 2008, the University of Michigan Library was in the process of moving its library website to Drupal 6. Prior to this point, our website was a collection of HTML files, PHP code, and other items. We had no consistent design or structure. There were three different tools used to create guide-like content: two independent custom PHP applications and a set of HTML templates. As we planned our work, we realized that re-creating guide-like functionality was beyond the scope of what we could manage. So we decided to consolidate these three independent tools into the LibGuides product.

Following the decision to consolidate content in LibGuides, we faced the challenge of determining how to place guides in the library website in a way that would make them easy to find when sought but not more prevalent than they needed to be. The information architecture of the new Drupal website was based largely on the organization of schools and departments across the campus. This system became the driving force behind several search and discovery tools, including a new books tool (www.lib.umich.edu/newbooks), a mechanism to match subject specialists to user search queries, an Academic Discipline catalog facet, and a series of browse pages (www.lib.umich.edu/browse).

We knew it would be important to integrate LibGuides into the existing frameworks of the library website. Additionally, we observed a strong desire from library staff to place more library-generated content within CTools, the university's Sakai-powered LMS. To achieve these goals, we decided to provide access to LibGuides content in three places within the library website and to create an automated workflow to provide appropriate subject and course guides in the university's LMS.

LIBRARY WEBSITE INTEGRATIONS

We use our library website to expose our guides in search results, browse results, and staff profiles. To develop these points of integration, we came to an arrangement with Springshare to obtain a weekly export of our LibGuides system data. The data were provided as an XML file—a standard format for representing hierarchical data, in plain text, through the use of consistent tags to indicate labels for the data. This XML file reproduced Springshare's database structure and included information such as a guide's title, its authors, tags, and content, in separately demarcated lines. Though we had the full content of each guide available in the export, we decided not to ingest it all to reduce weaker matches in our site search. On a weekly basis, we would ingest each guide's metadata for title, author, tags, and description into a Solr (lucene.apache.org/solr) index to facilitate searching. Solr is an open-source indexing tool that is designed to work with XML or other fielded data. It allows us to search on specific fields and adjust their relative relevance weight, making it a flexible and customizable search tool for the library website.

Search Results

When users submit queries through our site search, they're presented with search results from LibGuides in the right-hand sidebar of a bento-box-style interface as

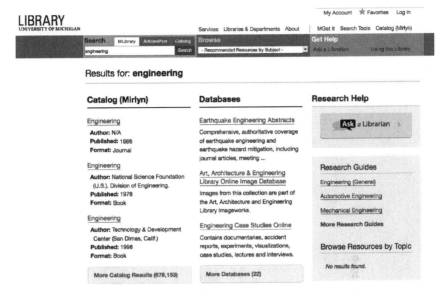

Figure 3.1. Search results displaying guides related to engineering.

depicted in figure 3.1. This placement keeps guide results separate from our most frequently used search targets, while making them available to people searching explicitly for them. The site search can be used to retrieve guides relevant to a specific course, academic discipline, or topic. Only the guide title is displayed.

Browse Results

While our initial exports of LibGuides XML data contained the information needed to match individual guides to a site search, they did not contain the metadata needed to associate guides with a controlled vocabulary of browse categories. We considered building an application to track extra metadata separately from LibGuides' native interface. With a separate application, guide authors would be able to edit guide content normally in LibGuides and edit a list of relevant browse categories for each guide in another website. We decided that the extra burden on guide authors, of maintaining guide information in multiple locations, would have outweighed the benefits of using a fully supported controlled vocabulary. Instead, we applied tags to guides to record this information.

When users browse our library website, they're prompted to select one or more of 257 browse categories. After making a selection, they're directed to a bento-box-style interface that includes results from LibGuides in a prominent second column as shown in figure 3.2. Up to three guides, with truncated descriptions, are displayed by default.

When more than three guides are associated with a browse category, users can view a lengthier results page that separates guides into two sections: Highly Recommended and Other. An example can be found in figure 3.3.

LIBRARY
UNIVERSITY OF MICHIGAN
My Account
Favorites
Log in
Services
Libraries & Departments
About
MGet It
Search Tools
Catalog (Mirlyn)
Search
MLibrary
ArticlesPlus
Catalog
Search
Browse
- Recommended Resources by Subject -
Get Help
Ask a Librarian
Using the Library
Home > MLibrary Browse > American Culture
Browse results for: American Culture
Online Journals
American studies
The American historical review
The --
More Online Journals (3268)
Databases
MLA International Bibliography
Indexes books and articles published on modern languages, literatures, folklore, and film.
Research Guides
United States History
This guide covers major resources and methods for research in U.S. history. Some of the key resources discussed in th...
Museum Studies
Provides useful resources for research on museum studies.
British and American History
Provides resources, strategies, and information on conducting research in British and American history.
More Research Guides (5)
Research Help
Ask a Librarian
Talk to a Specialist about American Culture
Alexa L Pearce
Librarian for History & American Culture

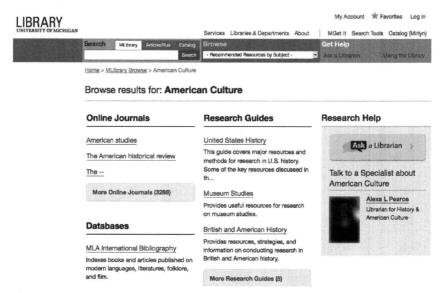

Figure 3.2. Browse results displaying guides related to American culture.

The browse associations are controlled entirely by tags. All of the guides shown in figure 3.3 appear because they contain the tag *international_studies*. The first nine guides appear as Highly Recommended because they include the tag *best_bet*. The tagging guidelines we developed include underscores because LibGuides has not always supported tags containing spaces. Because the tags are added manually, we have

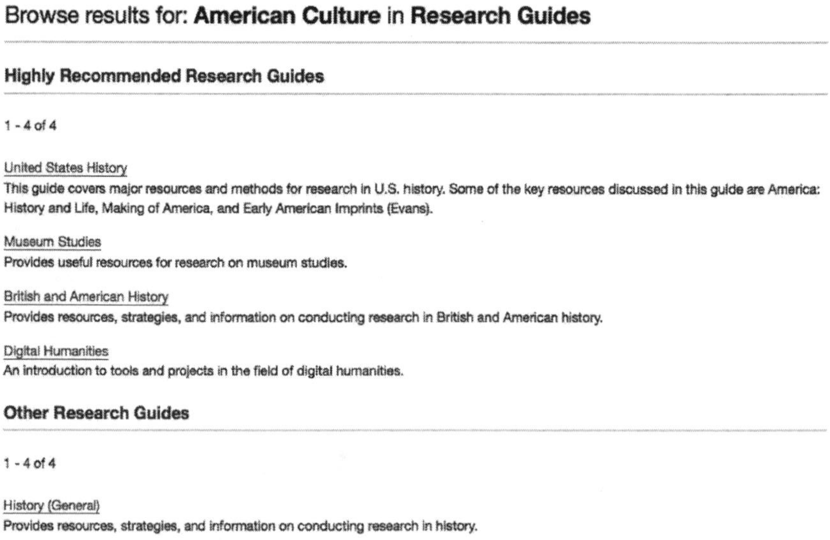

Browse results for: American Culture in Research Guides
Highly Recommended Research Guides
1 - 4 of 4
United States History
This guide covers major resources and methods for research in U.S. history. Some of the key resources discussed in this guide are America: History and Life, Making of America, and Early American Imprints (Evans).
Museum Studies
Provides useful resources for research on museum studies.
British and American History
Provides resources, strategies, and information on conducting research in British and American history.
Digital Humanities
An introduction to tools and projects in the field of digital humanities.
Other Research Guides
1 - 4 of 4
History (General)
Provides resources, strategies, and information on conducting research in history.

Figure 3.3. Extended browse results for guides related to American culture.

encountered challenges related to scope, such as guides appearing in the wrong category, and syntax—guides not appearing because a tag is malformed or misspelled.

Staff Profiles

Our third LibGuides integration within our site involves staff profiles. Users viewing a profile encounter a list of guides authored by that staff member. Figure 3.4 shows what this looks like. This information is updated as often as we ingest data from LibGuides. Guides will only appear if the staff member is the primary guide owner. Collaboratively authored guides not owned by the staff member do not appear.

Figure 3.4. Profile displaying guides authored by a staff member.

LMS INTEGRATIONS

CTools (Sakai)

The first version of LibGuides did not include tools for integrating content with CTools, our university's Sakai-powered LMS. Consequently, we developed an LTI-compliant tool for retrieving guides associated with specific courses. LTI, or Learning Tools Interoperability, is a standard method for one system to provide information to another. The LTI standard specifies formats for sharing information of particular value in academic settings, such as course names and numbers, departmental affiliation, and more. It is also the standard way to include external data in our campus's LMS, where students view their course syllabi and reading lists, interact with faculty, submit their homework, and view their grades. The tool is a single-page website that receives input in a clearly defined format and provides HTML as output. As with the library website browse pages, this integration is dependent on metadata placed in tags. A single tag indicating that a guide should match a specific section of a course might look like *subject:english course:125 year:2015 term:fall section:097.*

Adding a guide to a CTools course requires a course designer, or an instructor/authorized delegate with appropriate access permissions, to add a tool called Research Guides to the course site navigation. The tool is automatically configured with basic information about the course to which it has been added (e.g., subject, course number, section, campus, term, and year). It then queries our university registrar's office for the name of the course's instructor and the list of any courses cross-listed with it. The tool then matches against the tags for the most specific combination of subject, course number, section, term, year, campus, and instructor. This requires that the subject matches, but any of the other course attributes are allowed to be more loosely matched. For example, a guide can be designated to match any English course by professor Smith (*subject:english instructor:smith*) or only section 097 of English 125 in the fall term of 2015 (*subject:english course:125 year:2015 term:fall section:097*).

When this works successfully, course participants who access the tool from course site navigation are presented with a page containing a hyperlink to the relevant subject or course guide. We show this in figure 3.5. If a matching guide isn't found, a link to the LibGuides homepage appears instead.

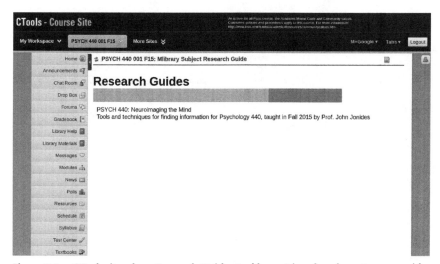

Figure 3.5.   CTools site where Research Guides tool has retrieved a relevant course guide.

Canvas (Instructure)

When the University of Michigan announced it would begin a transition to Canvas, an Instructure-powered LMS, library and campus IT stakeholders agreed it would be advantageous to provide course designers with a LibGuides tool similar—if not identical—to the one appearing in CTools. While the tool the library developed for CTools is LTI compliant and should work in every popular LMS, we chose to explore other options for initial Canvas integrations.

Shortly before the campus began transitioning, our library migrated to a new version of LibGuides (LGv2). The new version included an LTI tool that, when enabled, would permit course designers to embed LibGuides content (e.g., entire guides, individual pages, or boxes) in course modules or assignments. This is shown in figure 3.6. We worked with our LMS administrators to enable this tool across campus. Features of an LTI tool, such as links for course site navigation, are provided to an LMS with an XML file.

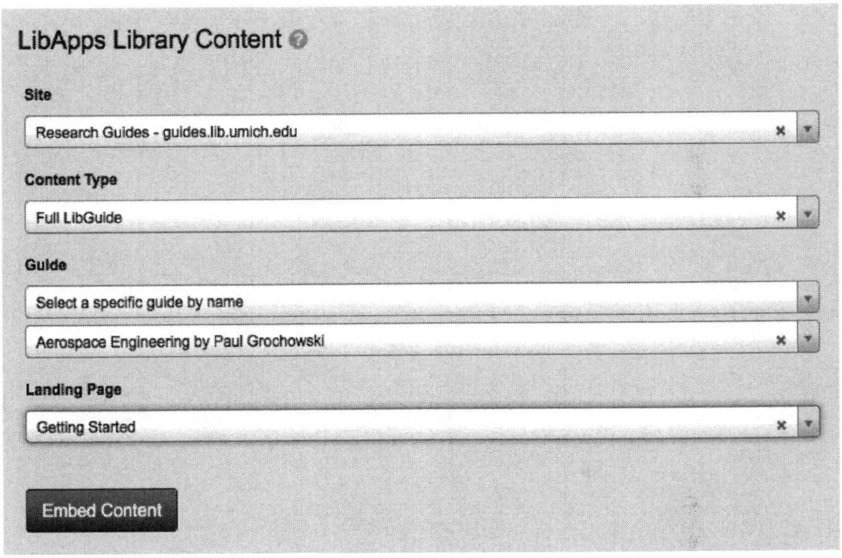

Figure 3.6. Selection options for embedding LibGuides content in Canvas.

The vendor-provided LTI tool we've integrated with Canvas has notable differences from the tool we developed for CTools. Instead of matching a relevant guide to the course site by default, it requires a course designer to manually select the content they would like to display. Instead of launching content in a new window, it launches within the same frame of the course site. We are still exploring the capabilities of this tool, as well as the possibility of implementing our CTools tool within the Canvas environment. We have also met with Springshare to provide feedback on their LTI tool based on our experiences.

CHALLENGES AND OPPORTUNITIES

Running LibGuides as a content management solution for a subset of our library's web content opens up a number of opportunities, as well as presents a number of challenges. A significant challenge is that we are simply running two content management systems. Our library website has search interfaces to our licensed content, books, and discovery services. It also has information about our physical locations, collections, services, and staff. Our instance of LibGuides has subject-specific information that includes links to subject-focused databases. Aside from the duplicated technical overhead of managing user accounts and permissions in two distinct places, this can lead to user confusion about which site to use and what content is properly sought in which service. We have tried to resolve this by presenting LibGuides content in relevant places within the library website, but the dual services still present user experience challenges.

We have attempted to minimize the impact of these challenges through interface design. Our LibGuides and library website have different visual themes but appear as members of the same graphic family and share a common set of navigation links. Over time, we have repeatedly tweaked the CSS stylesheets in LibGuides and minimized content authors' ability to add colors, fonts, and other elements. Ensuring consistency of the interface across the library's web presences helps provide an aura of quality beyond the actual words on the page.

Furthermore, LibGuides content provides access points to the broader library website, with direct access to our library catalog and other discovery tools (e.g., the article, database, and journal finders). An Ask a Librarian chat widget is present in both sites, which provides a continuity of in-person service between them. We suspect that students are less aware of the library's brand when they view our LibGuides as opposed to our other online sources. We hear from faculty that they appreciate seeing the library brand and knowing they can trust the information. They also indicate that they understand that links to full-text licensed content will therefore work seamlessly.

Our next significant challenge is that the overwhelming majority of LibGuides usage comes from Internet search engines and not the library website. Between January and April 2015, which closely corresponds to the University of Michigan's winter term, Google Analytics reports that there were 466,221 user sessions. Of those, nearly 83 percent (386,718) originated with Internet search engines. Google alone accounted for 375,305 of those sessions. Of the remaining user sessions, 48,462 (10.4 percent) came from direct links, leaving only 29,311 (about 7 percent) of user sessions originating from all other sources. Links from the library (e.g., the main website, catalog, etc.) accounted for 19,512 sessions—slightly more than 4 percent of total sessions—with the remaining 9,799 coming from other campus websites.

Google Analytics reports that 43,981 sessions (9.4 percent of the total) originated in Ann Arbor, Michigan, the home of the University of Michigan. While not all U-M students, faculty, and staff are in Ann Arbor, this seems a reasonable proxy for usage by U-M affiliates. More than half (53 percent) of U-M LibGuides usage came from an impressive 224 countries other than the United States. These usage statistics raise questions about the intended and actual audiences of this large swathe of content.

The way we index LibGuides content on our main website may provide part of the answer. As noted above, we currently index only the high-level metadata for each guide (e.g., title, author, subject, tags, and description). This does not include the full text of the guide's content. We rely more heavily on the guide's subject to trigger its appearance in a particular location as part of the Research Help section or a browse page.

CONCLUSION

We have used LibGuides for eight years as of February 2016. Our library's migration to LGv2 required us to reevaluate our existing LMS integrations. Additionally, the migration enabled us to improve some of the website integrations we had already developed. Whereas we previously worked with Springshare to obtain weekly XML data exports, we now use tools within LGv2 to export LibGuides data and reindex it in our website on a daily basis. We are also exploring options for using LGv2 features for adding internal metadata fields to replace our current practice of placing browse category and course-related metadata in public-facing tags.

Reflecting on the website and LMS integrations we've developed during that time, we've learned that—for institutions using LibGuides as more than a stand-alone website—dramatic improvements in guide discovery and access can be made relatively quickly and at low cost. Some of the integrations we've mentioned in this chapter were developed and implemented by individual library staff, while others were completed by small teams. It has been helpful for us to have access to many staff members with a wide range of technical expertise; however, we believe these integrations can be replicated by significantly smaller organizations.

4

Leveraging LibGuides as an EZProxy Notifications Interface

Jason Bengtson, MLIS, MA, Kansas State University

Libraries regularly struggle to reach their full user base with announcements and alerts. This chapter describes a unique solution to this problem adopted by the Texas Medical Center Library in Houston, Texas. The library's "proxyFu" application pushes announcements out to our EZProxy login page. The user interface for the tool, built in LibGuides, allows librarians with little or no technical skills to create announcements. This allows the departments generating the announcements to create attractive messages quickly and easily.

BACKGROUND

At the first Texas Medical Center (TMC) Library Operations Team meeting of May 2015, it was clear that the library had a communications problem with its patrons. There were a number of staff members at the meeting that favored creating an announcement vehicle for outages or similar situations that could be more prominently featured on our homepage. This was due to a recent library resource outage that had left the public services librarians scrambling to answer angry questions, despite the library pushing notifications about the event through its various existing communication channels. The library possessed an active social media presence, which it was able to leverage in such circumstances. However, this strategy was only able to reach that fraction of library users interested in engaging with the library through social media. Further, library website announcements were slightly buried in a drop-down menu.

I wasn't convinced that changes to the homepage were the answer. Internal library considerations complicated the process of altering the website significantly. Additionally, the library used Google Analytics to track website activity. Google Analytics is a free application that works by adding a small amount of JavaScript to the webpages institutions wish to track. Shortly after arriving at the TMC Library the previous month, I had significantly enhanced the library's ability to track user interactions through the introduction of several levels of "custom events." These custom events required more JavaScript but provided us with granular statistics about everything from click events to scroll events employed by our users in interfacing with our site.

The statistics we had already culled, and which we refined over the next few months in order to confirm our initial findings, were clear. Almost none of the library website visitors were looking at announcements—and almost all of them were immediately seeking out databases. This led to the suspicion that most of our site visitors were using our website as little more than a path for database access. Many others, I believed, just bookmarked the databases they wanted. This was borne out later when I added Google Analytics to our EZProxy login page and our regular website. There was already a drop-down menu for announcements on the homepage, and click events on those announcements were almost nonexistent. The homepage was unlikely to be our most effective announcement vector.

I noted that there was a superior alternative: EZProxy. The TMC Library is unique in that we are the library of record for several educational institutions but we are not formally attached to any of them. All library users, even when on-site, are required to sign in to EZProxy for resource access. This is so that costs could be calculated and apportioned between member institutions on a use-proportional basis. Given that our Google Analytics numbers pointed toward a user base that employed our website almost exclusively as an entry point to database and eBook resources, it seemed clear that pushing announcements out to the EZProxy login page was our best option. While these could mirror the announcements on the library website, there was no need to limit them as such. There was also no reason to limit the announcements to emergencies.

This project involved two departments who served as the main stakeholders: Customer Relationship Management—which handled classes, reference, systematic reviews, and liaison duties—and Resources Management. The latter is responsible for licensing, cataloging, and assuring the availability of the library's information resources. After consultation with these departments, it was decided that a variety of announcements could be deployed. These included classes, new product announcements, and other items of general interest to users.

There was significant interest in this approach by the Library Operations Team, and I was asked to build a proof-of-concept app for purposes of evaluation. Fortunately, the library possessed a development version of EZProxy, set up as part of another project, where the idea could be safely tested and rolled out for evaluation.

METHODS

Pushing announcements out to the EZProxy login page presented several challenges. I would be writing the code, but I would not be the service owner. The tool would need to be built to allow librarians with little or no web coding skill to author announcements. In other words, the tool would need to be a web app that separated web code—such as HTML, CSS, and JavaScript—from content. It would also need to provide librarians with a user-friendly editor that they could employ without requiring the intervention of technical staff or a great deal of additional instruction.

The obvious interface for this purpose was LibGuides. Reference librarians at the TMC Library were already familiar with it and its built-in What-You-See-Is-What-You-Get (WYSIWYG) editor. This was the editor that allowed librarians to create box content in LibGuides without using HTML or CSS. I decided that, by building a simple LibGuide with editable boxes for creating content and changing announcement attributes, I could put together a highly librarian-friendly front-end for the announcement tool. I built the interface as a private LibGuide, so that supervisors could easily control editor access to the app. The interface itself was quite simple. An editable box was designed to hold the actual announcement. Changes to text color, the addition of lists, and other textual formatting could easily be accomplished via the WYSIWG editor that the TMC librarians were already used to using. There was no "switch" for turning announcements off and on; rather, only when the app detected content would it generate an announcement on the EZProxy login page.

Other boxes were used to set additional visual features. One box contained a line of text that read, "To change the background color of the announcements, change the color of this text." It worked exactly as advertised. Another box accepted a number between one and three for positioning the announcements. Yet another box allowed the author to set one of two effects to further draw the user's eye to the announcement. The first available effect was a venetian-blind-style movement, which caused the announcement to "roll up" and then "roll down" again. The second effect was a gentle cycling of the color of the announcement border. There was also a box showing screenshots of the different announcement positions to serve as a reference for announcement authors. Once the configuration was established, another box contained a button that, when clicked on, would push the changes out to the app.

Though the interface guide itself was easy to build, I was left with a larger problem. EZProxy and LibGuides existed in completely separate silos. The library controlled EZProxy and the server it was installed on but had no control over the LibGuides server. LibGuides not only existed in a separate domain, it was also hosted externally and we had no server access to that hosted environment. I needed to find a way to effectively and reliably bridge the gulf between the two.

My answer to this challenge was building a PHP script which captured the HTML of the LibGuide, by use of the client URL (cURL) library, before teasing out the content and settings added to the boxes by librarians. PHP (Hypertext Preprocessor) is a scripting language similar in some ways to JavaScript but designed to run on a web server. The cURL library is a library designed to allow PHP to communicate with many other kinds of servers on the web. The script carved these elements out through the use of regular expression (REGEX) matching, a mechanism supported by many languages that allows for very flexible selection and replacement of text.

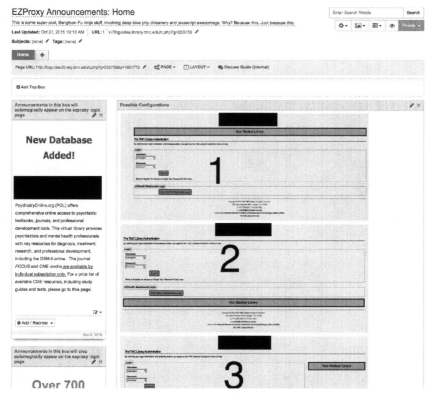

Figure 4.1. A screenshot of part of the current version of the proxyFu LibGuide interface.

This PHP script was built on the library's new applications server, positioning it—digitally speaking—between the LibGuides and EZProxy servers.

After the data was extracted, it was dynamically written into a JavaScript file and outputted to the same server. From there it could be loaded into any webpage. A simple script element added to the EZProxy login page loaded the JavaScript. In order to avoid situations in which editors might forget to push their changes out to the login page, I added the PHP script to the crontab (a scheduling mechanism that exists on Linux servers) on the app server, scheduling it to run every ten minutes. The script itself, including line breaks added for whitespace and internal commenting, is about 259 lines long. The TMC Library is currently investigating options for a mechanism to make this code available to other interested parties.

The JavaScript file averages about 177 lines when it is generated. Once the script is loaded into the login page, the JavaScript uses Document Object Model (DOM) constructors to dynamically generate the announcements box and populate it. These are special mechanisms, accessible to JavaScript, that allow for new webpage elements to be created. This makes it easy to not add the announcement element to the webpage if nothing has been supplied from the LibGuide user interface. It also allows the tool to degrade gracefully so that, in the relatively unlikely event that a visitor has JavaScript turned off in their browser, there will be no trace of announcement elements appearing on the login page. This mechanism also makes the overall user interface more intuitive. If there is no announcement saved to the announcement box, nothing will populate into the EZProxy login page. There are no additional radio buttons to check or confusing selections to make in order to "activate" a saved announcement.

Graceful degradation is carefully built into the tool on multiple levels. One consideration, from the beginning of the engineering process, was creating an interface that would degrade gracefully in the event that a user accidentally entered the incorrect input to one of the attribute boxes or any other interface element. As such, the PHP script was written to look for specific values from the attribute box contents and, should nonstandard or nonmatching values be found, replace them in the JavaScript file with default values.

DEPLOYMENT

After initial testing in the development environment proved successful and the partner stakeholders were satisfied with the 1.0 version of the tool, it was certified for deployment by the chief operating officer and pushed out into the production EZProxy environment. A new LibGuide was created to interface with it so that there would be a separation of development and production on the input side of the equation as well as the output side. The departmental service owners had to establish their own standards for content and approval. We formed a proxyFu implementation team to expedite this process and provide a feedback loop for continuous development of the tool. The team consisted of myself, Beatriz Varman (the head of Client Relationship Management), and Joanne Romano (the head of Resource Management).

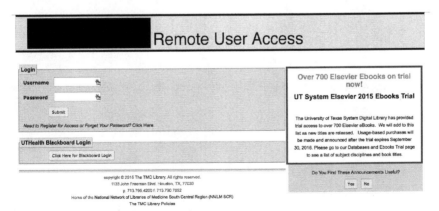

Figure 4.2.   A screenshot of the EZProxy login page with a proxyFu announcement in the side (3) configuration.

At this point in the project, there was a clearly defined separation between development and production, as well as code and content. Initial use of the tool proved highly successful. The other team members established workflows and a chain of approval within their departments for announcements. Staff members in both departments would approach their department heads with announcements that they wished to see pushed out, and Joanne and Beatriz would decide together if they believed the announcement merited deployment via EZProxy. The announcements would first be crafted and tested on the development version of the tool and then, upon approval, be ported to the production version. Additionally, Joanne and Beatriz could also generate announcements as needed.

The other team members also requested small changes to proxyFu's appearance. This included adding CSS to prevent any overflow incidence and altering the border color of the announcements box. Feedback from internal stakeholders, identified as staff members involved in the process of generating announcements, was consistently positive.

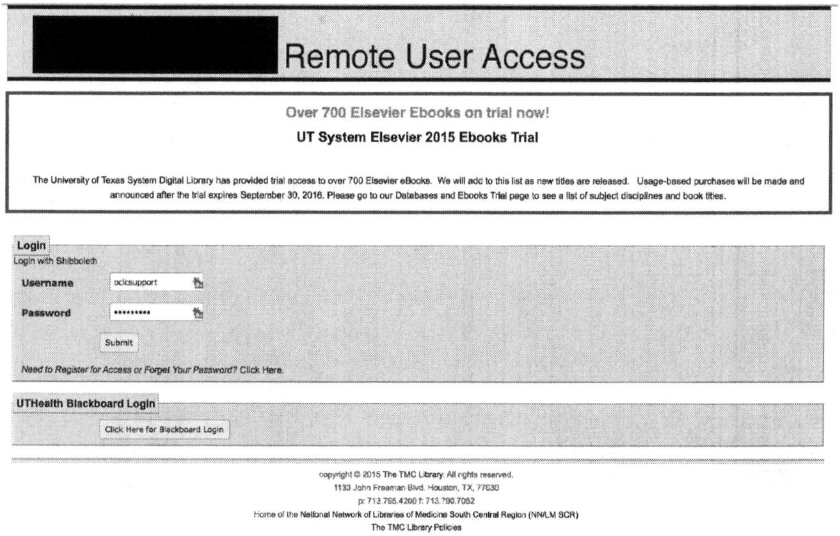

Figure 4.3. A screenshot of the EZProxy login page with a proxyFu announcement in the top (1) configuration.

After several weeks of use, my teammates agreed that it would be useful to be able to generate multiple announcements in the interface and asked me if there was a feasible way to do this. We discussed various strategies, eventually deciding upon a system of three announcement creation boxes in the LibGuide interface, with a pseudo-random number generator in the JavaScript determining which of the announcements the user would see upon visiting the page. In the original version of the tool, the alert creation box was tested for content to see if there was anything to display. The new 2.0 version followed the same pattern—adding alerts that were extracted from the LibGuide to an array (a special feature in JavaScript that can hold many changing values) from which the pseudo-random selection would be made. As such, it wouldn't matter how many alerts had been generated or even if any had been added to the LibGuides interface at all. As with proxyFu 1.0, in the absence of any announcement HTML, the tool simply didn't generate any announcement box on the EZProxy login page. Librarians could create up to three announcements or they could have none at all. The announcement boxes didn't need to be filled in any particular order. And no special knowledge was required to make the tool work properly.

ASSESSMENT

Assessment was integral to the proxyFu development process at all stages. Google Analytics usage data from the library website had already formed much of the basis for the proxyFu strategy. With proxyFu's deployment, assessment of visits to the login page, as well as any assessment of engagement that could be reasonably acquired, would be essential to getting an effective picture of utility. The first step in providing the basis for assessment was to add Google Analytics to the login page so that user movements, particularly clicks on the announcements, could be tracked effectively.

Page analytics confirmed that significantly more users were visiting the EZProxy login page than were visiting the library's homepage, but it quickly became apparent that—unsurprisingly—users didn't tend to click on the announcements. Simple page navigation gave reliable statistics on the number of sessions in which announcement content was delivered to the library user base, but the project team members were interested in finding ways to contrast engagement between the proxyFu announcements and announcements on the library website.

The proposition was difficult, especially given that the comparison was bound to be intrinsically incompatible. The website announcements were located in a drop-down menu on the website. Analytics indicated that many drop-down events regularly occurred to anchors in this menu in a random enough distribution that significant numbers of the events were probably due to relatively unfocused cursor movements by users.

The only useful way to measure engagement with the website announcements was to measure click and scroll events. All of these happened only after the user had, intentionally or inadvertently, actuated the drop-down announcement list. In addition, the click and scroll events had to be measured by "unique" events rather than by overall event quantity. Unique events, in Google Analytics, are a measure that counts one event on a webpage object per a user's visit to a site, no matter how many times they fire that event. Using unique events allowed the team to try and tie a particular user to an event, rather than measuring an aggregate of events, which could have been the result of a small number of users interacting with the announcements many times. This was particularly problematic with scroll events, where one "episode" of scrolling through the list of announcements could show up as many separate scroll events.

Even when examining unique events, the potential for the same users to have actuated at least óne unique scroll event in addition to one unique click event on the announcements was quite high. It was probable that a user would scroll through some of the list before clicking on an announcement item. Given the casual nature of scrolling, the utility of these events in proving user interaction compared to actual click events was limited. The announcement drop-down contained brief announcement summaries so I decided to use scroll events in addition to clicks as a comparative element.

On the EZProxy login page, all visitors were exposed to the announcements, but it might not occur to them to click on the announcements for more information. As a "honey pot" to attract engagement, I added a small survey that appeared below the announcement and fed its click events directly into Google Analytics. Asking users, "Do you find these announcements useful?" with yes and no response buttons, the survey was deemed relatively useless for general feedback data. The proxyFu team decided that the sample size would be too small and the respondents too self-selected to provide statistically relevant data. However, if it attracted clicks, it could provide a primitive basis for engagement comparison with the website announcement data.

The results of the comparison were interesting. From June 1 to August 31, 2015, there was a total of 183,307 total sessions on the library website. There were 194,190 sessions on the EZProxy pages during that same period. Further, there was a total of 629 unique scroll and click events on the website announcements. The overwhelming majority of these were scroll events.

In contrast there were a total of 591 unique click events on the EZProxy announcement during that same period. Subtracting clicks from the overall website announcement events, based upon the assumption that users who clicked through to see the full announcement had also engaged in at least one scroll event, brought the totals even closer: 605 website events to 591 EZProxy events.

Comparing only click events on the EZProxy announcements to click events on the website announcements, on the other hand, drew a stark comparison. Over the period in question, there had been only 24 clicks on the website announcement links, in contrast to 165 clicks on the actual EZProxy announcements.

The results seemed clear. In a measure of aggregate unique events, interactions in both formats were remarkably close. In a measure of click events, proxyFu announcements were the clear winner by a wide margin. And in terms of sheer exposure, the number of unique user sessions in which proxyFu announcements were served up dwarfed any similar measure, including raw sessions, from the library website.

CONCLUSION

Through all versions, feedback from stakeholders has been consistently positive. The tool has provided a reliable, easy-to-use platform for delivering announcements to the library's users. It has successfully separated code from content, allowing librarians with limited technical skills to create, modify, and deliver web-based announcements via a mechanism that has, by virtue of the unique position of the TMC Library at the medical center, achieved broad saturation of the library's user base. As such it has been judged a success by the library, and a regular cycle of evaluation and development is already under way for the app, to ensure that it continues to be properly maintained and reimagined.

II

LEARNING MANAGEMENT SYSTEM INTEGRATION

5

Strategies for Success

Building LibApps in Moodle
That Students Will Use

*Lydia Willoughby, MLIS, MA, State University
of New York at New Paltz
Meghan L. Dowell, MLIS, Beloit College*

State University of New York (SUNY), Plattsburgh launched a library resources block, in the campus Moodle learning management system (LMS), during summer 2015.[1] At this time, Plattsburgh was also migrating to LibGuides version 2 (LGv2). Moodle is an open-source LMS similar to Blackboard. It is built on pedagogical principles of constructivism to facilitate student interaction and collaboration in online courses, blended learning, and flipped classrooms. A block in Moodle is a small application within the larger LMS that can be thought of as a widget. Our library resources block serves as a course- and subject-specific application that connects students, in Moodle-supported online courses, to effective research guides using a widget for LibGuides relevant to their course site. It was created by a team that included librarians, programmers, instructional designers, and information technologists. Similarly, Beloit College migrated stand-alone webpage research guides to LGv2 in fall of 2014. A team of three librarians led the task to evaluate and prepare the best templates for the students. The librarians realized embedding the guides into their Moodle instance would be beneficial for students and faculty in online courses.

This chapter contains a side-by-side comparison of two institutions—one baccalaureate and one master's largely based on Carnegie basic classifications—in which both completed successful integration between LibGuides and Moodle. We'll detail how each library has enhanced student success within Moodle-based courses and how we augment face-to-face classes by providing readings, presentations, quizzes, and asynchronous discussions. Strong planning and collaboration among librarians and other departments were integral at both institutions to the design and implementation of successful tools based on LibGuides/LibApps. This helped make library resources both usable and relevant to faculty and students at their point-of-need.

LIBGUIDES/LIBAPPS AND MOODLE

Initial Steps

At Plattsburgh and Beloit, before planning could begin, a "librarian role" needed to be created in Moodle to allow clear communication of instruction goals for online instructors and students. This role allowed "just-in-time" library instruction linked to in-person sessions, course assignments, and online discussion. When added to Moodle courses by the instructor, librarians in this role can add custom research guides, post research examples, and guide discussion in online forums. The main distinction between this and the "instructor role" is that the librarian role cannot view student grades or assignment submissions.

Another consideration for Plattsburgh was that the SUNY system announced the launch of Open SUNY in early 2013 (State University of New York 2013). Open SUNY is a portal to view and register for online courses available at all SUNY campuses offering online programs. For programs to be included in Open SUNY, library support for online courses needed to be secure and fully integrated and available to online and distance students.

Proof of concept at Plattsburgh began with consulting library peers at institutions that successfully integrate library resources in learning management systems with customized widgets (Brewer, DeFrain, and Kline 2013). We found that highly customizable design is preferred and should be based on minimalist user experience principles so that students can find what is relevant at their point of need. "Students who use library guides delivered through a LMS find the guides useful. . . . However, direct librarian involvement with the course is not required to reach students and have a positive outcome on their learning" (Murphy and Black 2013, 528–34). Instructors should be able to modify what research guides are displayed, request new research guides, or opt out of the service entirely. Additionally, blocks should be content aware, so their default setup aligns with the course discipline. Custom links to citation help and style guides should also be available.

Plattsburgh consulted with the University of Arizona Libraries, as they have a library super widget that embeds course-specific resources in online classes and is designed to reach as many students as possible. The design principle of reaching students with information became an important part of our process. York University Libraries have a library box that allows instructors to replicate LibGuides content with a tag that can be linked in Moodle. For automated library content to be displayed, instructors are tasked with copying and pasting the HTML code generated by the tag (York University Information Literacy Steering Committee 2014).

Oakland University successfully merged the discovery search application Summon with SubjectsPlus research guides to automatically generate library content for Moodle (Hristova 2013). As with York University, Oakland instructors have to copy and paste HTML code into Moodle to make this work. Plattsburgh felt that this was a barrier—multiple steps would lessen the possibility of online instructors adopting the integration of library resources in Moodle.

Concordia University has a default library block that is content aware and is preloaded with course reserves, recommended databases, ask-a-librarian service, individual interlibrary loan, and account access (Concordia University Libraries 2015). It is an extension of the library liaison program, and this idea was central in Plattsburgh's design planning. Even more crucial, the Concordia block is integrated in all Moodle courses by default. This principle of inclusion and opt-out deletion meant that there were fewer steps and barriers to instructor adoption. For the block to be included in all Moodle course sites by default, dynamic content appropriate to discipline and subject was necessary. Additionally, instructors needed to be able to customize the block in some ways.

Strong campus outreach was important to completing this Moodle block project at Plattsburgh. The stakeholders included librarians, programmers, instructional designers, and information technologists. Additionally, faculty members invested in online learning were included for collaboration and feedback on the initial draft. Specific design approval was presented to the campus Faculty Teaching, Learning, and Technology Advisory Group.

Proof of Concept

Figure 5.1 shows our proof of concept based on the design examples considered earlier in this chapter. The initial draft included a discovery search box of discipline-specific catalog and database resources, a research guide for the corresponding discipline, a citation and working-with-sources link, and a link to a guide on plagiarism and an academic integrity tutorial. Also included in the initial draft design was an

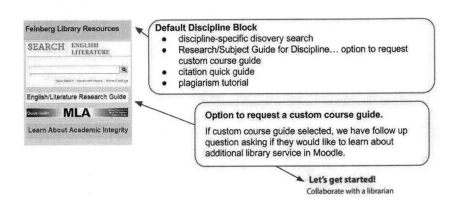

Figure 5.1. The original proof-of-concept draft design of the library resources block in Moodle at SUNY Plattsburgh.

option for course instructors to request a custom course guide. If "custom course guide" was selected, the form would display a follow-up question asking if the instructor would like to learn about additional library services in Moodle.

Next Steps

At Plattsburgh, the key to integrating dynamic content into Moodle was working with a programmer from computing systems. Collaboration on design iteration resulted in a user-friendly final product that allows the instructor to easily configure the library resources block, assign a liaison librarian to the Moodle course site, and delete the block entirely if desired. In order to customize the block, the instructor can configure the block to edit or add links to LibGuides and citation help URLs. Additionally, an instructor can assign a librarian to make changes or updates to only the library resources block in the Moodle course site.

Plattsburgh and Beloit both utilize the widget function in LibApps to display research and course guides in Moodle. Relevant courses are displayed as clickable options to the user instead of clunky HTML code that a user needs to copy and paste.

Dynamically generated content finds the most relevant resources for each unique course at the point of need for students and displays it. Our design choices were influenced by the goal of having LibGuides used as often as possible. In migrating to LGv2, we saw that use was highest for "research guides" (i.e., the guides that focused on the department level). Murphy and Black have written about how lowest-use LibGuides are at the course level (2013). Based on these design considerations, we focused time on editing department-level guides.

New guides requested by faculty fit into a liaison program that helps to keep course guides up to date on a semester by semester basis. As with Beloit, implementation of the widget from LibApps means that guide URLs have to be restricted to describe only guides currently in use at Plattsburgh. A clean up of LibGuides URLs was conducted as part of the migration to LGv2, with attention to parsing distinctions (e.g., libguides.plattsburgh.edu/art, libguides.plattsburgh.edu/ART, libguides.plattsburgh.edu/Art101). Because a librarian role had already been established prior to library resources block design, they could administer the block and the URLs linked via the LibApps widget. For the library resources block to function in Plattsburgh's Moodle instance, a "LibAdmin" account was set up to manage the updates for new guides—such as new URLs—so that they could be listed among the options visible to users. LibAdmin had to be set as a librarian role in the Moodle course site.

Instructors can customize the content and look of their library resources block in Plattsburgh's Moodle instance, allowing integration of library resources as well as access to information across disciplines. This is especially useful in an interdisciplinary seminar. Customization of content and guide display helps students to focus on the information most relevant to their assignments and studies. The library resources block connects students to useful research guides and allows the course instructor to modify what research guides are displayed, request new research guides, or opt out of the service entirely; the librarian can edit the library resources block. but the instructor has final edit and approval of all content. Figure 5.2 is a hypothetical illustration of the history of bluegrass music—focused on West African influences—with a customized link to the citation builder at North Carolina State University.

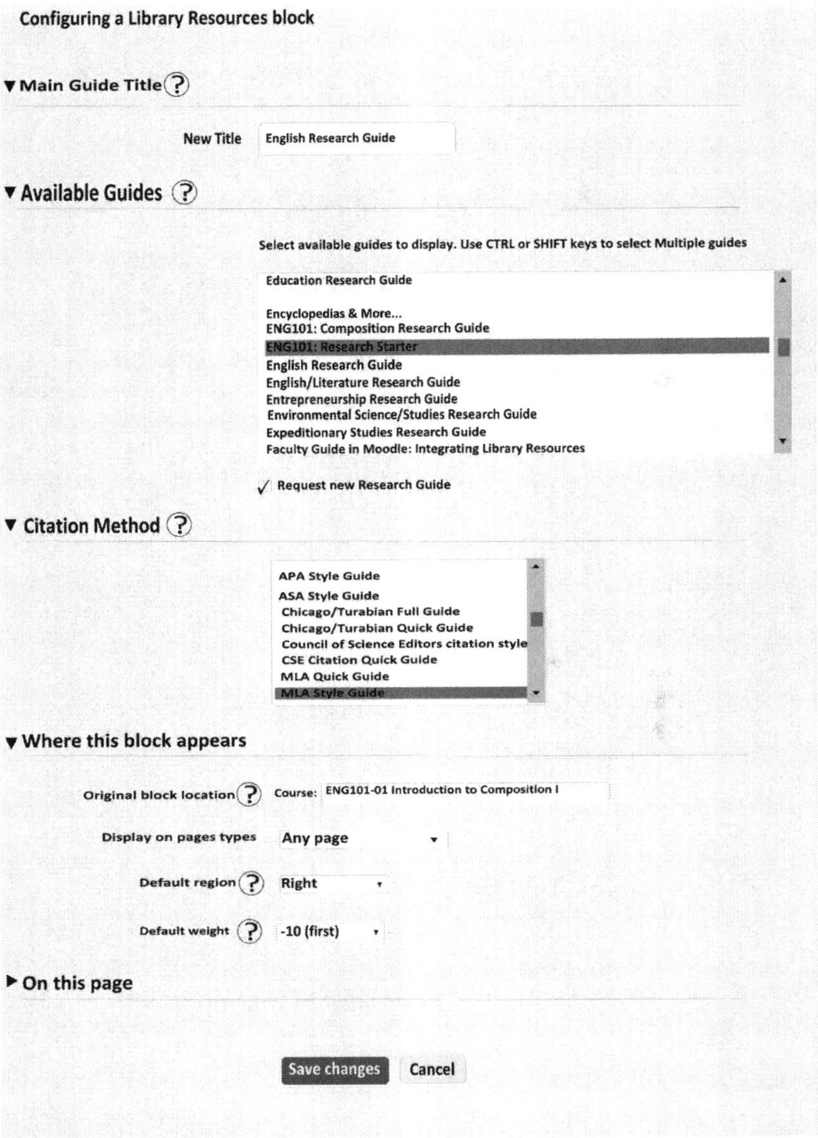

Configuring a Library Resources block

▼ **Main Guide Title** (?)

New Title   English Research Guide

▼ **Available Guides** (?)

Select available guides to display. Use CTRL or SHIFT keys to select Multiple guides

Education Research Guide

Encyclopedias & More...
ENG101: Composition Research Guide
ENG101: Research Starter
English Research Guide
English/Literature Research Guide
Entrepreneurship Research Guide
Environmental Science/Studies Research Guide
Expeditionary Studies Research Guide
Faculty Guide in Moodle: Integrating Library Resources

✓ Request new Research Guide

▼ **Citation Method** (?)

APA Style Guide
ASA Style Guide
Chicago/Turabian Full Guide
Chicago/Turabian Quick Guide
Council of Science Editors citation style
CSE Citation Quick Guide
MLA Quick Guide
MLA Style Guide

▼ **Where this block appears**

Original block location (?)   Course: ENG101-01 Introduction to Composition I

Display on pages types   Any page   ▾

Default region (?)   Right   ▾

Default weight (?)   -10 (first)   ▾

▶ **On this page**

[Save changes]   [Cancel]

Figure 5.2. An example of a customized interdisciplinary course's use of the library resources block, showing a link to multiple LibGuides and a link to an external citation builder.

Figure 5.3 is what the library resources block might look like in an information literacy class on critical research skills.

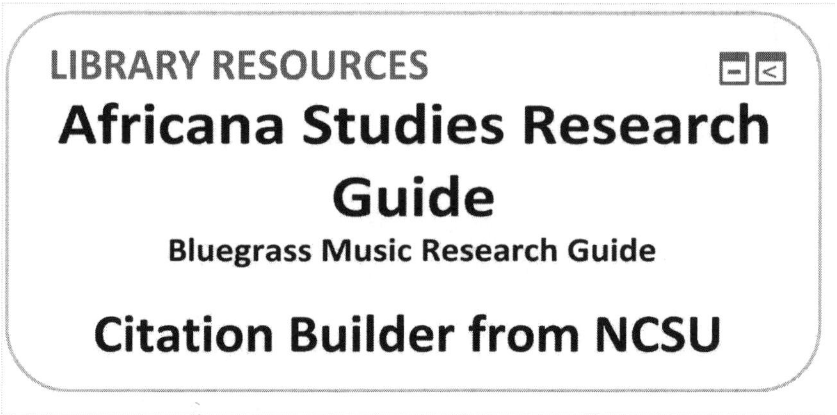

LIBRARY RESOURCES   ⊟ ◁

Africana Studies Research Guide
Bluegrass Music Research Guide

Citation Builder from NCSU

Figure 5.3.   An example of the library resources block for an interdisciplinary course, set only to the list of research guides by topic on the library's homepage.

Compare figure 5.3 to figure 5.4 to see how a traditional English 101 general education course's library resources block might appear.

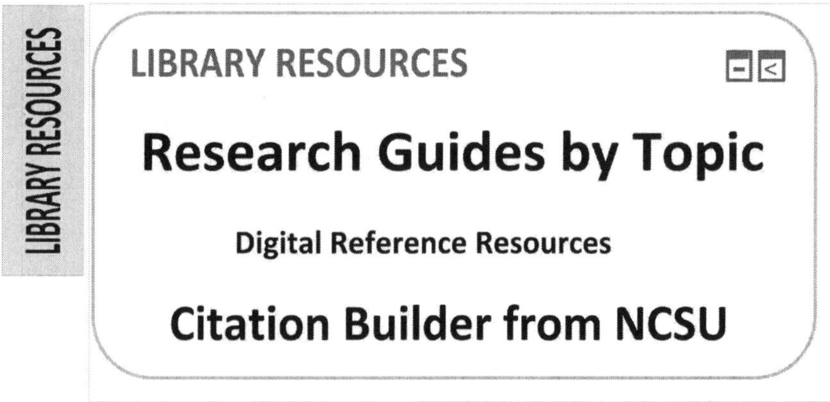

LIBRARY RESOURCES

LIBRARY RESOURCES   ⊟ ◁

Research Guides by Topic

Digital Reference Resources

Citation Builder from NCSU

Figure 5.4.   An example of the SUNY Plattsburgh library resources block set up for an English 101 course.

Marketing

At Beloit College, Instructional Technology (IT) is located in the library and shares office space with librarians. This intentional arrangement was created to encourage collaboration between the two groups. IT worked with our librarians on two fronts in Moodle. The first was to create a Marketing Block with an embedded widget of the Subject guide drop-down list. This is meant to promote LibGuides. The drop-down subject guide list is created in the LibGuides widget creator by choosing the Subjects tab, then selecting the criteria to complete the drop-down. Figure 5.5 displays the widget customizations made at Beloit College.

Figure 5.5.   Suggested selections to make in the LibGuides widget creator.

The Marketing Block displays on every page of Moodle, outside of course pages, as shown in figure 5.6. The librarians stressed the importance of creating a highly visible library block before the students reached their course pages.

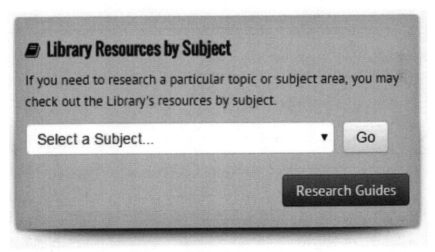

Figure 5.6.   The subject widget in use on Beloit College's Moodle.

Secondly, IT created a role for librarians that gave them editing powers to embed course or subject guides into Moodle courses. There are two other locations in Moodle where the library has space prior to the student or faculty member entering their course. These are in the top header, a custom library block with contact information, and as the drop-down Subject guide selector.

DISSEMINATING LIBGUIDES/LIBAPPS KNOWLEDGE INTERNALLY

Beloit College had many guides to create, dividing roughly thirty programs between three librarians in a small liaison program. We ensured consistency in navigation, created subject and course templates, and conducted usability testing before making final edits to these templates. Internal training was provided to teach the LibGuides interface and stress the importance of best practices.

Course and subject templates were created to establish continuity between the librarians and our interdisciplinary students. Templates were created in phases. First, sample templates were created by using best practices compiled by librarians on the Information Literacy Instruction listserv (Wood n.d., 1–9). These were discussed by the liaison librarians to determine the best combinations for our campus. Once those were decided upon, the librarians began to complete the subject and course guides as requested. Usability testing commenced after the LibGuides interface had been live for a few months. Recommended changes were slated to be made over the following summer.

Beloit College took suggestions from the Metropolitan State University case study on user-centered design in LibGuides (Sonsteby and DeJonghe 2013, 83–94). The usability testing began by one librarian reading a scripted question, asking students to locate where a journal article might be linked within a subject guide. This allowed the monitoring librarian to take notes on what was happening on the screen and being said aloud. The takeaways helped to develop a sense of how students understand the heading and labels. Next, the students were asked to recommend changes and even offer suggestions on how to rearrange the subject guide to better suit their needs. The key finding from this exercise: add better navigation to the homepage.

Asset maintenance within LibGuides can be an overwhelming task. However, proper maintenance allows for mass changes to be a simple process. For instance, to update search boxes from OCLC WorldCat Local to OCLC Discovery, the library utilized the search and replace function within LibGuides. Alternatively, if one asset is mapped to multiple pages, the librarian can edit the asset and push the changes to all of the mapped guides. An integral part of asset maintenance is reusing content that has been previously created. Utilizing content created at the home institution, or even requesting permission of completed guides at other institutions, can save time and reduce duplication. Plattsburgh also employed this strategy of mapping LibGuides changes to keep content in Moodle relevant and up to date. Final design considerations and realities of the discovery search at Plattsburgh resulted in us dropping discovery search for discipline-specific library resources from the library resources block.

EMBEDDING RESEARCH GUIDES AT POINT OF NEED

Approximately 50 percent of the faculty at Beloit College use Moodle to accompany their face-to-face courses. Through liaison collaboration, librarians meet with a variety of classes to instruct on research and other information literacy skills. At Beloit College, general practice is that after the librarian has an instruction session with a class using Moodle, we embed the subject or course guide into the class Moodle instantiation. The faculty have the ability to move the widget or link to meet their needs. This allows the students to reference handouts and topics discussed in the instruction session without leaving their course interface. Beloit College found a 275 percent increase in embedded guide usage versus a guide that has not been embedded. The students have grown to expect their needs be met quickly—providing an access point in an environment where they work has proven successful (Daly 2010, 208). Additionally, though it took time for the requests to begin, both institutions have several faculty that take advantage of this service and customized course guides have grown in use every semester.

Library anxiety has been well documented (Mellon 2015, 276–82). Liaison programs, however, help lessen the complexity of connecting with a subject librarian. LibGuides provides the space to create an interface where students can simply access library resources, organized by discipline, and begin to answer some of their first level questions. Beloit College librarians have utilized the Profile box to provide general contact information and also a link to their You Can Book Me (youcanbook.me) schedule. The library liaison program is also beneficial to new faculty on campus. The LibGuides URL is provided for onboarding and orientation. This helps connect users to the library at their point of need.

Library resources block assessment at Plattsburgh found that of the 737 active Moodle courses in fall 2015, 712 (97 percent) had a library block in their course site. This high rate of implementation indicates that the block design was successful in connecting students, and instructors in online classes, with direct access to the library resources and research guides they needed. One percent of faculty constituted the 3 percent of Moodle courses that opted out of the library resources block entirely.

SUNY PLATTSBURGH'S FINDINGS

The only course-specific guide among the top used, within Moodle course sites, is our Social Work 304 guide. Social work majors often take SWK304 in the fall semester of their senior year; it is required for graduation and is research intensive. "This course is both writing intensive and one in which writing is an integral/intrinsic part of the learning process. This course meets the advanced writing requirements for the Social Work Department" (SUNY Plattsburgh 2010). As an "advanced writing" course that is "writing intensive," the presence of a course-specific library guide integrated with the learning management system is an obvi-

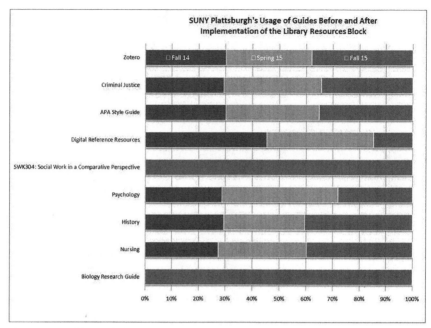

Figure 5.7.   This graph shows the usage rates of LibGuides before and after implementation of the library resources block at SUNY Plattsburgh.

ous way to connect students to critically useful library resources at point of need. Usage rates are displayed in figure 5.7.

Due to the requirement and the timing, it makes sense that this guide would have a high rate of usage, and it is telling that there is no use of the guide prior to the implementation of the library resources block in Moodle. This indicates that its adoption in Moodle course sites is connecting senior-year social work majors to the critical library resources they need to complete research-intensive coursework. As shown in figure 5.8, most of our guides increased in usage after implementation.

Our psychology program encompasses an undergraduate major and minor and a graduate program in school psychology. In the spring semester, many of the psychology courses feature labs, upper-division requirements, and advanced graduate courses that require more research. Thus, library instruction is higher in spring for psychology courses. The actual rate of use in fall 2014 is comparable to rate of use in fall 2015, especially considering that the fall 2015 semester is still under way (at the time of writing).

In the fall of 2014 and spring of 2015, the Digital Reference Resources page had a very prominent display on the homepage of the library website and was the primary mode of access for all of the library reference databases at Plattsburgh. Responding to usage and user demand, in fall 2015, a new search layer was added to the library collections search option on the library homepage. This change added the ability to

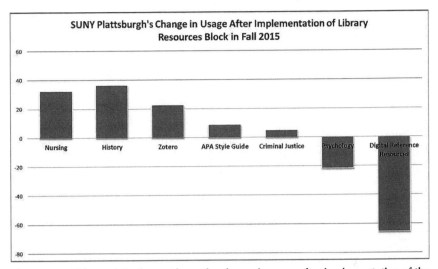

Figure 5.8. This graph further analyzes the change in usage after implementation of the library resources block in fall 2015 at SUNY Plattsburgh.

search reference resources directly from the search box. These user design changes are reflected in the higher usage of the Digital Reference Resources page in fall 2014 and spring 2015, as well as the seeming dip in usage in fall 2015. In reality, more people are using these resources now, though they are no longer accessing them through the Digital Reference Resources page.

The Zotero guide is primarily used in workshop and classroom instruction and has been well supported through instructional programming for students and training for faculty. This page remains a frequently used resource on campus due to continued librarian outreach, promotion, and support for Zotero training and installation. Though the Zotero guide is not affiliated with any one specific course, faculty have the option to customize their library resources block in Moodle, and Zotero is among the options available. There was a 23 percent increase in Zotero page usage after the block's implementation. This demonstrates the success of word-of-mouth campus outreach and promotion, as well as online point-of-need service for students and instructors in Moodle.

Tracking LibGuides usage by semester is much more useful if finals and the associated end-of-semester research assignments are included in timely analysis. Nevertheless, this snapshot of usage in late November 2015 shows important increase in the LibGuides associated with core academic disciplines at Plattsburgh. The nursing program, in particular, is part of the new Open SUNY program, and its online courses all feature access to library resources through the library resources block in Moodle. Further, we saw a 36 percent increase in history usage of LibGuides. The majority of these courses are blended or face-to-face.

The power of point of need speaks to the presence of biology and a social work course site pages among the top used guides in fall 2015. Previously, biology courses at Plattsburgh did not receive any library instruction that included library resources connected to their Moodle course sites. The specific cultural and demographic research resources necessary in comparative social work requires connecting these students to resources that they can use—when they need them.

Future assessment of this and other projects integrating library resources in learning management systems could address:

- qualitative surveys of faculty views on use of library resources in student research,
- the impact of outreach and promotion on use of library resources by students,
- the impact of outreach and promotion on the use of library resources by faculty, and
- the correlation of embedded library resources in the learning management system to the integration of information literacy and complex usage of library resources in course assignments and syllabi.

CONCLUSION

Although Beloit and Plattsburgh used the same tools to integrate library resources in online education—LibGuides and Moodle—these examples demonstrate that using the same tools does not mean that the end result will be the same. We've shared successes in increased collaboration between libraries and faculty. And, as shown earlier in this chapter, Plattsburgh has shown marked increase in resource usage after integrating LibGuides and Moodle. At Beloit College, connecting the Moodle class space to the Library's LibGuides has allowed conversations to take place that increase collaboration between faculty and librarians. Specifically, faculty have taken an active role in helping to select materials featured in the course guides. We have also experienced an increase in usage by integrating the guides into Moodle instantiations. Though it is too early for evaluation, Beloit College is witnessing higher subject-specific database usage due to LibGuides and Moodle. Students' perception of library relevance may have also improved due to the availability at their point of need: this is an opportunity for our own future research. Generally, though, more research needs to be done regarding aligning student perception and availability of resources at point of need. Anecdotally, students are commenting on the ease of finding specific journals and databases and that it is leading them to create better final research papers. Due to these results, we will continue our partnership between Instructional Technology and librarians to keep improving services.

It is critical that library instruction encompasses how students can use the resources in LibGuides to make the library relevant to their needs. The design of putting LibGuides directly in Moodle course sites has always been about connecting users at their point of need—this reduces barriers to access and increases the timeliness of LibGuides as a research tool. Outreach and training on how users can incorporate library resources into campus scholarship remain vital to the success of any online integration project, and is important for classroom instruction, blended, and online learning.

NOTE

1. This chapter focuses on Moodle integration. However, many of the ideas presented are easily adaptable to other learning management systems.

REFERENCES

Brewer, Michael, Erica DeFrain, and Elizabeth Kline. 2013. *Stanford Prize for Innovation in Research Libraries Nomination January 2013.* Tucson: University of Arizona Libraries.

Concordia University Libraries. 2015. "Introduction." Library Resources Moodle Block. library.concordia.ca/services/users/faculty/moodle/.

Daly, Emily. 2010. "Embedding Library Resources into Learning Management Systems: A Way to Reach Duke Undergrads at their Points of Need." *College & Research Libraries News* 71(4): 208. search.proquest.com/docview/203793245.

Hristova, Mariela. 2013. "Library Widget for Moodle." *Code4Lib Journal* (19). doaj.org/article/d41764b5cbc34af4ae00970bdfd7dc57.

Mellon, C. A. 2015. "Library Anxiety: A Grounded Theory and its Development." *College & Research Libraries* 76(3): 276–82.

Murphy, Sarah Anne, and Elizabeth L. Black. 2013. "Embedding Guides Where Students Learn: Do Design Choices and Librarian Behavior make a Difference?" *Journal of Academic Librarianship* 39(6): 528–34.

Sonsteby, Alec, and Jennifer DeJonghe. 2013. "Usability Testing, User-Centered Design, and LibGuides Subject Guides: A Case Study." *Journal of Web Librarianship* 7(1): 83–94.

State University of New York. 2013. "History of Innovation." Open SUNY. open.suny.edu/about/history-of-innovation/.

SUNY Plattsburgh. 2010. "SWK304 - Social Welfare in Comparative Perspective (3 Cr.)." Search the College Course Catalog. www.plattsburgh.edu/php-bin/catalog/crs.php?q=swk304.

Wood, Sarah. (n.d.) "LibGuides Best Practices." Pierce College. docs.google.com/document/d/1Ph X6dwCKnCJdjQgjE2kHJeyY56RXAZ4b8QiiTkq49Go/edit?hl=en&authkey=CKyOoosD.

York University Information Literacy Steering Committee. 2014. "E-Learning—Moodle." Resources for Instruction Librarians. researchguides.library.yorku.ca/resources_instruction_librarians.

6

Using LibGuides as a Learning Management System

An Exploratory Study

Sharon Whitfield, Rowan University
Susan Cavanaugh, Rowan University
Catherine Marchetta, Rowan University

A learning management system (LMS) provides an array of tools and features to support instruction. These tools include asynchronous and synchronous communication (e.g., announcements, e-mail, chat, and discussion boards), homework collection, and formative and summative assessment (e.g., multiple choice testing and instructor feedback). Yet, few face-to-face instructors use an LMS for instructional/assessment purposes or to foster community within their classes (Woods et al. 2004). Existing commercial LMSs, such as Blackboard, may have very practical constraints for face-to-face instruction. For example, LMSs tend to be cost-prohibitive or university policies may restrict use to authenticated users only. Additionally, face-to-face instructors primarily use LMSs more like a content management system (CMS). Their activities include publishing, editing, and modifying instructional documents or supplementing face-to-face instruction (Woods et al. 2004). The LibGuides technology allows for the functionality of a CMS and has features that offer some asynchronous communication tools such as discussion board and comments. This chapter discusses how Cooper Medical School of Rowan University (CMSRU) utilized LibGuides as a substitute LMS. We will also analyze the potential of LibGuides, as a replacement for a more traditional LMS, to deliver instructional documents and supplement face-to-face instruction.

BACKGROUND

CMSRU welcomed twenty students into their inaugural MEDAcademy program in 2015. MEDAcademy is a four-week summer day program that provides students, interested in the field of medicine, the opportunity to explore it through lectures, hands-on demonstrations, and interactive and clinical experiences. These are taught by CMSRU's faculty, medical students, and staff. Each week students rotate through one of four medical specialties: cardiology (week 1), neurology (week 2), pathology (week 3), and gastrointestinal systems (week 4). The program is rigorous; it requires students to review Grand Round lectures and Active Learning Group case objectives and prepare for lectures with readings. Due to university policies, these students were not authorized to access Blackboard, which is the CMSRU LMS.

MEDAcademy program directors consulted with the emerging technologies librarian to find a solution. The faculty and students needed a technology that would aid in content delivery, as well as track and manage program content, in order to support the rigors of the MEDAcademy program. After discussing programmatic needs for course content delivery, the librarian suggested use of an existing library technology—LibGuides—as an alternative to a traditional LMS. LibGuides is a CMS that allows librarians to organize and present information using Web 2.0 technologies.

For the past year, CMSRU Library has utilized LibGuides as "portal pages" for medical specialties (rowanmed.libguides.com/cmsru). The portal pages have been well received by the CMSRU community. In fact, in a recent CMSRU usability survey, a respondent acknowledged that topic-specific resource guides were their "favorite website features." Each portal page is collaboratively developed with a librarian and a member of clinical faculty, biomedical sciences faculty, and other professionals. The collaboration allows librarians to aid in selecting the best resources for a specific subject area. The portal pages primarily contain links to e-resources, websites, and contact information. They do not, however, contain many of the LibGuides "Web 2.0" technologies, such as RSS feeds, embedded multimedia, and asynchronous communication tools. The CMSRU librarians decided to explore other LibGuides functionality to determine whether LibGuides would be an adequate replacement for an LMS. Partnership with the MEDAcademy program was an opportunity to support the program and explore this area.

After agreeing to utilize LibGuides in lieu of a traditional LMS, the MEDAcademy program directors and the CMSRU librarians began to exchange e-mails regarding account permissions, access to licensed library resources, how LibGuides could be used to supplement face-to-face instruction, limitations of using LibGuides, and training/support for MEDAcademy. This helped to outline an action plan for how we would proceed.

ACTION PLAN

The MEDAcademy action plan consisted of action steps that would support the MEDAcademy program's use of LibGuides. These included creating a MEDAcademy LibGuide, creating MEDAcademy facilitator accounts, providing training and support for users, and creating content.

Creating the MEDAcademy LibGuide

The MEDAcademy LibGuide was created by the emerging technologies librarian. Initially, this included a home page that would be used for program-wide announcements, a page for each of the four medical specialties addressed (e.g., cardiology, neurology, pathology, and gastrointestinal systems), and a Books page to provide on-campus access to library resources. A Discussion Board page, available in LibGuides CMS v1, was later added to promote asynchronous communication among facilitators and students. The MEDAcademy LibGuide publication status was made private, assigned a friendly URL that would make it more memorable to users (e.g., rowan.v1.libguides.com/2015medacademy), and password-protected to limit access to only intended users.

Creating Facilitator Accounts

The MEDAcademy program directors supplied a list of individuals who would be acting as MEDAcademy facilitators. These facilitators were assigned as co-owners to the previously created MEDAcademy LibGuide. Each facilitator was responsible for the content within their assigned medical specialty week but could add, edit, or delete any text or boxes on the guide. Therefore, each facilitator had to trust that their peers would not edit or delete their respective content. An administrator account was also created for the MEDAcademy coordinator, allowing them to create accounts, create/edit pages, edit HTML, and change guide information.

Training and Support

The emerging technologies librarian had a brief one-on-one session with the MEDAcademy coordinator, due to heightened access permissions, on how to support the facilitators with account problems, HTML questions, and some style guidance. Additionally, CMSRU librarians provided facilitators with a three-hour instruction session that demonstrated:

- creating box content (e.g., text and links);
- adding documents;
- embedding multimedia;
- adding interactive polls, surveys, and user feedback;
- design and style guidelines;
- viewing guide statistics; and
- collaborative functions (e.g., discussion boards and commenting).

They were also given a general how-to handout about LibGuides creation and contact information for the emerging technologies librarian and the assistant director of CMSRU Library. The librarians provided few style or design tips during the training session and did not limit the look and feel of the LibGuide. This allowed MEDAcademy facilitators, many of whom were CMSRU students, to utilize their guide to enhance their pedagogy and supplement their face-to-face instruction as they desired.

Librarians anticipated MEDAcademy facilitator questions about creating content on their LibGuide. However, no questions were received. Periodically, the librarians would review the MEDAcademy LibGuide to ensure that the facilitators were not struggling with any design or style issues. If the librarians noticed any problems, they would proactively send tips (e.g., how to embed multimedia) and remind facilitators that librarians were available to assist them. On several occasions, the emerging technologies librarian would informally ask facilitators about their experience creating content. Their responses of "fun" and "easy" reflected how many of the CMSRU librarians felt as we began the LibGuides design process.

Creating Content

MEDAcademy facilitators added any resources or tools that would enhance the students' understanding of the face-to-face instruction covered each week. Content was also added to supplement and extend the students' knowledge about the weekly topics. Facilitators created links, added documents, embedded media, and used box colors to make certain items stand out.

FINDINGS

The librarians who supported MEDAcademy reviewed the LibGuide after the program ended. We examined which pedagogical tools were used to enhance face-to-face instruction, file usage statistics, and LibGuide limitations for the MEDAcademy program. Most of these items were selected for review due to statistics inherently provided by LibGuides; preliminary questions were added in order to provide knowledge of LibGuides limitations in this application.

Pedagogical Tools and Usage

Consistent with the work of Hintz et al. (2010), the MEDAcademy facilitators—who are also CMSRU students—designed LibGuides pages that had a simple and clean layout. The MEDAcademy LibGuide consisted of colorful boxes, text document files, and embedded multimedia. Figure 6.1 provides a view of the MEDAcademy LibGuide.

Web 2.0 features and asynchronous communication tools (e.g., interactive polls, surveys, commenting, and discussion boards) were demonstrated as possible pedagogical tools to enhance communication and receive student feedback. Librarians found, however, that the MEDAcademy facilitators did not utilize any Web 2.0 communication technologies to supplement their face-to-face instruction. Additionally, usage statistics demonstrated that the MEDAcademy LibGuide had a total of 1,856 views within a four-week period. Figure 6.2 provides a breakdown of this by page views.

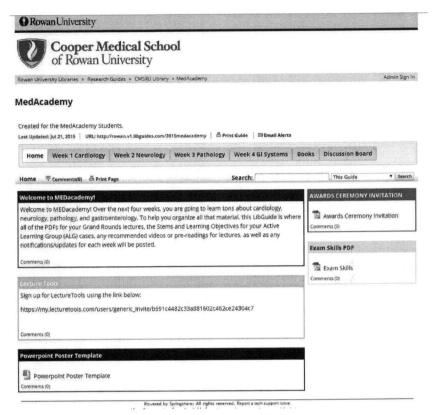

Figure 6.1.　Screenshot of the MEDAcademy LibGuide.

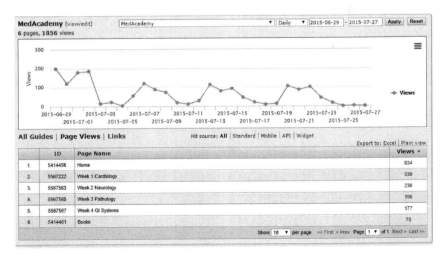

Figure 6.2.　Breakdown of MEDAcademy page views.

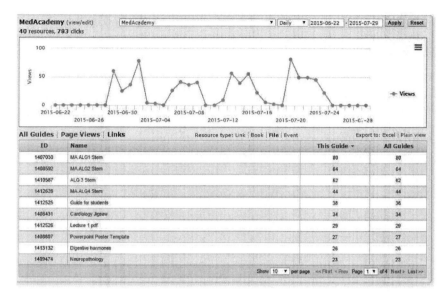

Figure 6.3.   File access statistics for the MEDAcademy LibGuide.

File access statistics, shown in figure 6.3, verified that students utilized LibGuides to access course content posted by faculty. There were no reports by facilitators that students' access was impeded in any way or that students could not access files.

LIMITATIONS

Librarians encountered limitations using LibGuides as an LMS to supplement face-to-face instruction. These included:

- Permissions on pages could not be restricted to an individual. This allowed everyone to edit/delete/add content to another facilitator's dedicated tab. Permission levels should be more granular to help with collaboration and allow for multiple people to work on the same LibGuide.
- Embedding multimedia was not clear cut. On the MEDAcademy LibGuide, two out of five videos extended past box borders. The video content was playable, but the look and feel of the guide was diminished. In order for the multimedia to display in the box correctly, the facilitators would have had to edit the dimensions of the embedded media within HTML. This is a daunting task to someone who has never coded or edited website markup.
- The attached 10 MB document file may be restrictive to documents that have media content. All MEDAcademy facilitators were warned that uploaded files must be below this limit. PowerPoints that had large images, animations, and

other embedded objects had to be saved to a web server location and then linked through the MEDAcademy LibGuide.

- No easy mechanism existed for taking down content. In order to be compliant with the Digital Millennium Copyright Act, content must be taken down after a course or program has ended. LibGuides does not have an easy mechanism for taking down content; therefore, each document must be taken down separately.

CONCLUSION

LibGuides functioned well for the MEDAcademy program and allowed facilitators to communicate with students effectively. We required content delivery to supplement face-to-face instruction, and in this way, LibGuides was successful. However, it had shortcomings that would inhibit its use as an institution's LMS and should not be used beyond the scope of a CMS. Further, an LMS should fulfill three goals:

1. provide students with digital learning materials;
2. employ interactive learning activities with students in the forums, wikis, and other collaborative tools; and
3. manage the course and the learners by maintaining tests, evaluating the students' learning and achievements, and giving grades online (Meishar-Tal et al. 2012).

LibGuides fulfilled the first goal of an LMS satisfactorily for the MEDAcademy program but was ineffective for employing interactive learning activities or managing the course and learners. Further, although facilitators were shown Web 2.0 technologies available in the platform, none of them promoted use of interactive learning activities in this way (e.g., discussion forums or commenting). After the course, facilitators stated that these technologies were not robust enough to engage students. The commenting technology does not allow for the student to format their text without knowledge of HTML. Furthermore, the commenting features could not control the targeted audience—the option to contact only a facilitator or only a select group of students was not available. Other LibGuides technologies, such as the interactive poll and user feedback, were also unfit to employ as interactive learning activities.

Since LibGuides is a CMS and not an LMS, there was no way to truly manage the course. Unlike an LMS that ties into a legacy enrollment system and adds registered students to the appropriate course, LibGuides only has the ability to password protect guides. Since students do not need to authenticate, facilitators do not know who is accessing the course or digital content. Therefore, facilitators do not know who is engaged in their course. Additionally, while testing on material is often used to determine engagement, LibGuides does not offer a robust assessment tool or a grading system. Therefore, we conclude that LibGuides is not a technology that can be utilized to determine if learning is occurring.

REFERENCES

Hintz, Kimberley, Paula Farrar, Shirin Eshghi, Barbara Sobol, Jo-Anne Naslund, Teresa Lee, Tara Stephens, and Aleha McCauley. 2010. "Letting Students Take the Lead: A User-Centered Approach to Evaluating Subject Guides." *Evidence Based Library and Information Practice* 5(4): 39–52.

Meishar-Tal, Hagit, Gila Kurtz, and Efrat Pieterse. 2012. "Facebook Groups as LMS: A Case Study." *The International Review of Research in Open and Distributed Learning* 13(4): 33–48.

Woods, Robert, Jason D. Baker, and Dave Hopper. 2004. "Hybrid Structures: Faculty Use and Perception of Web-Based Courseware as a Supplement to Face-to-Face Instruction." *The Internet and Higher Education* 7(4): 281–97.

III

DIGITAL COLLECTIONS

7

Using LibGuides to Build a Digital Museum Website

Scott Salzman, Furman University
Christy Allen, Furman University

"Art communicates so powerfully that it can make the impossible happen" (FurmanUnivLibraries 2014). Those are the words of Peter Wexler, renowned New York theater designer, producer, artist, and photographer. He was referring to the daunting task of creating the Peter Wexler Digital Museum at Furman University (hfurman.beta.libguides.com/wexler/home). In 2012, Wexler entered into a partnership with the Furman University Libraries to create the Digital Museum, a unique web-based exhibit showcasing the life's work of the artist. The Digital Museum project was led by the Libraries' Digital Collections Center and funded by a donation from Furman University trustee Todd Ruppert and his wife, Karen. Two staff members worked on the project full time over the course of three years—with contributions from two librarians and seven students and ongoing collaboration from Peter Wexler and his personal assistant.

The project team was able to plan and execute a truly innovative website despite the project presenting unique and complex challenges such as:

- The physical collection was very large; it contained more than thirty thousand individual items.
- The physical collection included numerous formats such as costume and stage designs, posters, three-dimensional models, photographs, VHS tapes, documents, CDs, and a six-foot stage backdrop.
- Staff resources and experience in managing large-scale digitization projects were limited.
- No widely accepted metadata standards for describing theatrical materials exist.
- All content in Wexler's collection is copyrighted by Wexler himself or by other photographers, artists, or theatrical groups.
- It was unclear which platform would best suit the particular requirements of the Digital Museum.

DIGITIZATION AND DESCRIPTION

The first step in creating the Digital Museum involved moving Wexler's artwork from his Manhattan studio to Furman's campus in Greenville, South Carolina. Initial estimates indicated that there were more than thirty thousand discrete items in the physical collection. Rick Jones, manager of the Digital Collections Center, was appointed the project manager. He has worked in libraries for more than ten years, including two years with the Digital Collections Center. He also has an MFA and a strong background in studio art. This project provided him with the perfect opportunity to leverage both his digitization knowledge and his artistic skills.

Approximately 7,500 items were selected for digitization after some basic physical collection processing. These items included all of Wexler's artwork, framed theatrical posters, and programs. The majority of the materials selected for digitization were oversized or three-dimensional and couldn't be digitized on a conventional scanner. Digital photography was the only solution, so we built a small photography studio in a conference room. We then purchased advanced lighting kits, spotlights, two backdrops, and a Canon Rebel EOS camera.

Rick Jones began photographing and training students to photograph. This wasn't a typical digitization project, so we used rather unconventional photography methods. Lighting and backdrops were used to create an artistic atmosphere and photographs were taken from all angles, with various lighting effects, to showcase the beauty of the artwork. In many ways, the digital photographs are as much artwork as the items they represent.

The photographs were shot in RAW. This is a file format often known as a "digital negative" due to its ability to be manipulated with minimal quality degradation. Next, the digital photographs were enhanced using Adobe Lightroom and Photoshop to improve color and lighting and to remove imperfections. The images were then saved as high-resolution TIFFs to prevent any loss of quality. Throughout the process, we were committed to presenting truly museum-quality photography in the collection, so a lot of our time was devoted to enhancing and preserving image quality.

Processed photographs were organized into projects. Each project contains all of the digitized artwork related to a specific Wexler job such as a play or opera. Items within each project were organized to reflect Wexler's creative process. In a typical project, the first files are rough concept sketches and the last files are photographs of the finished product. This chronological presentation provides an in-depth look into the creative process of an artist, allowing users to trace artistic ideas from unpolished concepts to completed works. Several professors of theater arts who have seen the Digital Museum claim this organization is the most important aspect of the website. It allows them to show their students the creative process in action.

Finally, quality control was conducted. Peter Wexler was an active participant and reviewed each project while offering suggestions for additional enhancements. After all the digital files were reviewed and approved, the TIFF files were used to create high-resolution JPEG derivatives for upload into CONTENTdm—Furman's digital collection management system. CONTENTdm is an Online Computer Library Center product characterized by its ability to quickly and easily create and customize digital collections. The system supports a wide range of file formats as well as the international metadata standard known as Qualified Dublin Core.

Developing metadata for the Digital Museum proved challenging. We chose to create two levels of metadata based on the Qualified Dublin Core schema. First, we developed project-level metadata, which applied to all items within a specific project. Examples of project metadata fields include: project name, date, client, and credits. Then we developed item-level metadata, specific to each individual digital image, such as title, format, media, and dimensions. We tracked the project-level metadata through a Microsoft Excel spreadsheet that was developed in collaboration with Wexler. We created the item-level metadata as we uploaded items into CONTENTdm.

SELECTING A WEB PLATFORM

The items were digitized, described, and made accessible on the web through CONTENTdm. However, the Digital Museum was far from complete. Christy Allen, assistant director for Discovery Services, and Scott Salzman, web discovery librarian, began the process of selecting an appropriate web platform. A major goal for the Digital Museum was to provide users with a website experience reminiscent of an art gallery. The benefit of using CONTENTdm is that it provides rich functionality. This includes highly customizable metadata, robust search capabilities, and zoomable images, all within the context of the complete collection. Unfortunately, this same richness results in a "busy" display that detracts from the artwork itself. After testing, we determined that CONTENTdm simply did not offer the customizations necessary to provide an online gallery experience. As such, it was not a viable option for hosting the Digital Museum website.

Other platform options available to us were Microsoft Sharepoint, LibGuides, and the library's legacy Apache web server. We rejected Sharepoint as an option because we did not have sufficient access to the university's Sharepoint server to do any customization. Our legacy Apache server was due to be retired, so building a sustainable website on it was simply not an option. Coincidentally, shortly after we began the search for a suitable web platform, Springshare announced the upcoming release of LibGuides version 2 (LGv2). This offered several compelling benefits.

We had a positive experience developing a customized website using LibGuides version 1 (LGv1), and thanks to its new template model, LGv2 promised to be even more customizable than its predecessor. In addition, LGv2 was built with the Bootstrap framework. This means that it supports responsive web design and our website could be made to work well on a variety of devices. Our experiences using LGv1, and other Springshare products, had shown them to be functional, easy to use, highly customizable, fast, and stable and to have responsive and efficient customer support.

As an added bonus, since we use LibGuides as the platform for our library website, we anticipated strong carryovers between our development of the Digital Museum and the upcoming migration of our library website into LGv2.

FUNCTIONAL REQUIREMENTS FOR THE WEBSITE

The first step in building the website was to determine our needs. As noted above, we knew that we wanted an art gallery feel to the website, so we opted for a simple design. Kathie Sloan, our digital projects specialist, working with Rick Jones, developed an uncluttered layout with a crisp black background as a means of showcasing Wexler's artwork. This simple design also proved to be readily adaptable to a responsive experience.

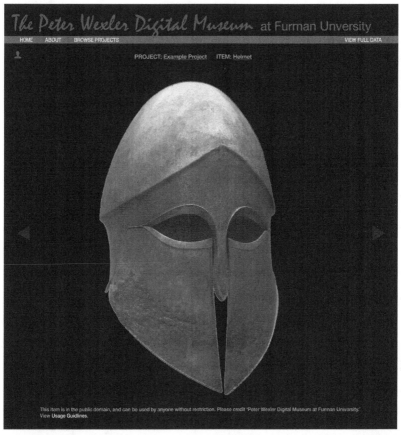

Figure 7.1. The Peter Wexler Digital Museum at Furman University website aims to convey an art gallery experience (this figure uses a non-project image for demonstration purposes). *Images of website created by Kathie Sloan and copyright © 2015 Furman University. All rights reserved*

We kept the website content simple and clean to fully capitalize on the "gallery feel." There is an "About the Digital Museum" page with background information about Wexler, the Digital Collections Center, and the Digital Museum itself. It serves as an introduction to the website and is reminiscent of the narrative you might find at the beginning of a physical museum exhibit.

The website also includes a list of projects, sorted chronologically, which allows users to browse by year or by project title. Selecting a project title opens a webpage containing the project-level metadata with descriptive information related to the project. From this page, users can link to the full project listing in CONTENTdm or they can preview selected items from the project. The preview pages were designed to provide users with the "gallery feel" noted previously. Each preview page showcases a selected item, in the form of a large image of Wexler's art, accompanied by just three metadata fields specific to that image: item title, project name, and copyright information. Users interested in learning more about an item can choose to view the full metadata and zoomable version of the image in CONTENTdm.

Finally, the last type of page on the website is a usage guidelines statement. All of Wexler's artwork is made available under the Creative Commons Attribution Non-Commercial Share Alike License 4.0. All other copyrighted items are viewable on the website, but reusing them is not permitted without written permission from the copyright holders.

In reviewing the functional requirements for the website, it became clear to us that the site would comprise well over a thousand webpages. Salzman has numerous other responsibilities and would not be able to create, update, and maintain such a large amount of web content for this project. As such, it was critical that the majority of the pages in the Digital Museum website be generated on the fly, by a script, rather than being manually created and saved as individual LibGuides. We accomplished this by building a custom "template" webpage and reusing metadata from CONTENTdm to populate it in different ways (described later in this chapter). Please note that our use of the term "template" here does not refer to LGv2 templates, but rather to our use of a skeletal webpage on which a locally developed script displays information or images related to a particular item or project. Due to the way that the site navigation works, the user experience is that of browsing through a large website containing several thousand pages.

WEBSITE COMPONENTS

Webpages

The entire Digital Museum website consists of just the following five physical LibGuides:

1. homepage;
2. About the Digital Museum page;

3. usage guidelines page;
4. Browse Projects page—a list of all the projects. A script retrieves a file containing project-level metadata and processes it to generate a list of the 197 published projects;
5. Project Details page—This page serves as the "template" for generating and displaying the following two different types of webpages.

   - 197 project landing pages—These pages are dynamically generated from both project-level and item-level metadata files.
   - 1,875 project preview pages—These pages are also generated from both project-level and item-level metadata files.

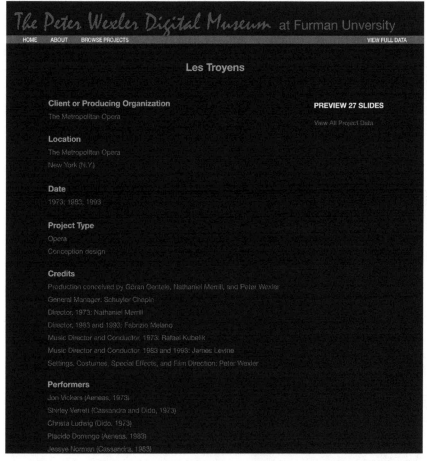

Figure 7.2.   The Peter Wexler Digital Museum at Furman University project landing page example. *Images of website created by Kathie Sloan and copyright © 2015 Furman University. All rights reserved*

Metadata Files

As noted earlier, we created two sets of metadata for the Digital Museum: project-level metadata, which applies to all items within a project, and item-level metadata, which is specific to the item itself. The project-level metadata is maintained in an Excel spreadsheet, and the item-level metadata is created and maintained in CONTENTdm. There is some overlap among metadata fields, with some of the project-level metadata incorporated into CONTENTdm to provide project context.

We knew that we wanted to leverage this metadata to populate the dynamically generated webpages that would comprise the majority of the Digital Museum website. It was fairly easy to work with the project-level metadata since it was stored in a spreadsheet and could be converted to other formats. However, one of the biggest challenges we faced was how to most effectively repurpose the item-level metadata that was stored in CONTENTdm. Initially, we investigated using the CONTENTdm application programming interface (API). This is a mechanism by which an external program or script can access the data stored by another website. Our tests indicated that retrieving metadata in this way, from our hosted instance of CONTENTdm, would not be fast enough to serve as the source for the data-driven website model we envisioned. Developing an effective model for reusing this metadata was a critical step in constructing the Digital Museum.

After researching, experimenting, and plotting out potential workflows, we determined that the best way for us to reuse the existing metadata would be to export it from CONTENTdm and convert it to a format that could be readily manipulated for display on a webpage. This has proven to be an efficient and viable strategy since the published metadata is fairly stable. The data format that CONTENTdm makes available for export is comma-separated value (CSV)—sometimes called "comma delimited" format—these files are often used to move data in and out of spreadsheets.

After we export the metadata from CONTENTdm in CSV, we use a web-based converter to reformat the metadata so that it can be more readily manipulated for use on a website. The data format that we chose for this purpose is called JavaScript Object Notation (JSON). This is a popular format for transferring and manipulating data on the web. It is a "lightweight" data format (e.g., there isn't much overhead mixed in with the data to maintain its structural relationships) that can readily be used to generate fast, data-driven webpages. We converted both the Excel spreadsheet project-level metadata and the CONTENTdm item-level metadata into JSON files. The following example of item-level metadata illustrates how straightforward JSON data can be:

```
{
    "Title":           "Chapter - Les Troyens",
    "Project":         "Les Troyens",
    "Copyright":       "Art and concepts copyright Peter Wexler. Digital
                        image rights held by Furman University. All rights
                        reserved.",
    "Identifier":      "1973_LesTroyens-001.jpg",
    "URL":             "http://our.contentdm.com/p16821coll1/id/882/rec/1"
},
{
    "Title":           "She wolf on opening night",
    "Project":         "Les Troyens",
    "Copyright":       "Art and concepts copyright Peter Wexler. Digital
                        image rights held by Furman University. All rights
                        reserved.",
    "Identifier":      "1973_LesTroyens-002.jpg",
    "URL":             "http://our.contentdm.com/p16821coll1/id/1568/rec/2"
}
```

Figure 7.3. The Peter Wexler Digital Museum at Furman University item-level JSON metadata example. *Images of website created by Kathie Sloan and copyright © 2015 Furman University. All rights reserved*

We also take the additional step of "minifying" the JSON files to maximize the rendering speed of our pages. The online minifier we use removes all of the white space from these files, making them smaller, so that they can be transferred and loaded more quickly from the LibGuides server into a user's web browser. Because the minified versions of these files are not very easy to read, we retain copies of the pre-minified JSON files to facilitate minor edits. We also implement such updates in the spreadsheet or in CONTENTdm, so that the next conversion or export will include these changes. We found that we could store the minified JSON files in LibGuides using the Documents/Files box type. This not only streamlined our workflow; it also made our website faster. It reduced the number of domains on which our content is stored.

Scripts

The scripts used to retrieve and process the metadata files are written in JavaScript and take advantage of the jQuery library that is available in LibGuides. A "library" is a collection of resources that make writing scripts or programs more efficient. jQuery is a popular JavaScript library that streamlines the process of writing scripts for manipulating content and adding custom functionality to webpages. Since Springshare incorporates jQuery into LibGuides, it was easy for us to use it in this project.

The scripts that we developed use a technique called AJAX to retrieve the metadata files. AJAX, Asynchronous JavaScript and XML, is a common web programming method for retrieving data that will be used to update parts of webpages. The term "asynchronous" means that the rest of a webpage will continue to load at the same time that the data is being retrieved. The reference to "XML" refers to the historical use of this data format, but it is now common to retrieve data in JSON format using an AJAX request. Once the scripts retrieved the metadata, we used standard JavaScript techniques for manipulating the JSON formatted metadata to repurpose it for display as webpage content. The scripts use the metadata to dynamically populate the majority of content on our website.

Images

We carefully developed an optimal balance between image quality and file size in order to ensure that the Digital Museum webpages loaded quickly. Initially, we hoped to reuse the images that were already stored in CONTENTdm as they were high-resolution JPEGs that offered excellent image quality and zooming capabilities. However, they contributed to slow webpage load times. We knew that we had to decrease the file size of the images while maintaining as much quality as possible to optimize performance of the Digital Museum. We decided that our best option was to store a copy of the images in the LGv2 Image Manager.

The first step in this process was to resize the images so that their pixel height and width were limited to the largest dimensions that would be displayed on the website. Not surprisingly, an image with smaller dimensions also has a smaller file size. Next, we compressed the images to 93 percent of their original quality using Google Picasa. Through trial and error and visual comparisons with the high-resolution JPEG files, we felt that this treatment yielded the best balance of image appearance and load time for the Digital Museum.

We also decided that, for the best security on this highly labor-intensive project, we would create a dedicated user account in LGv2 and store the optimized images in that user's personal Image Manager folder. This prevented anyone, except an administrator, from being able to manipulate these images within LibGuides.

Noteworthy Functionality

The Browse Projects page only contains the following static content: the page-level heading, the search box, and the footer. The list of links to the 197 published projects is generated by a script that first retrieves the project-level metadata file and then parses out the names and publication years of each project in order to generate the list of projects. The contents of the list are maintained through the external process of updating the project-level metadata in the Excel spreadsheet. The project links are styled to present large, tappable targets for users of touch devices.

Developing the projects list search functionality presented an interesting challenge. Since we did not have an external server available for this project, on which we might have installed a search engine and a dedicated database, our search options were limited to CONTENTdm or to what we could build within LibGuides. Using the CONTENTdm search functionality would have disrupted the art gallery experience we aimed to create in LibGuides, while the LibGuides search function could not be limited to search only our list of projects. We chose to modify a script that uses jQuery to search the contents of the HTML list that we generated from the project-level metadata. This afforded us complete control over the look, feel, and contents of the search results. Users can search by keywords in a project title or by the year of the project. The search function works by removing non-matching projects from the displayed list, so the "search results" are actually a filtered view of the generated list of projects.

The Project Details "template" page generates two different kinds of pages: the project landing pages and the preview pages. It is no surprise, therefore, that this LibGuide utilizes the most complex script logic on the website. This single LibGuide serves as a webpage "template," and a script retrieves both the project and item-level metadata files. This script uses the project-level metadata to display descriptive information about the project and also to change the web page's HTML title element so that a project-specific name will be displayed to assist a user in navigating among their web browsing history or any pages they may bookmark on the Digital Museum website. Since this one LibGuide is used to generate 2,072 webpages, it is important to provide the ability for users to determine which one of those pages they have viewed or bookmarked. If we did not do this, every bookmark or web browser history entry would display the name of the "template" LibGuide, and these entries would be indistinguishable from each other.

The script that generates the Project Details pages also makes use of the item-level metadata to display the number of "slides" in a project's preview. On the preview page, this same script dynamically displays metadata or information from the item-level metadata files. This includes: item title, project, copyright information, preview or "slide" pagination (e.g., "Slide 1 of 5"), and links to the items and projects within CONTENTdm.

As of October 2015, six of the 197 published projects had enhanced metadata that includes a narrative description of the creative process that Peter Wexler followed in developing those projects. Each of these projects include an icon on their preview pages that, when activated, displays "teaser text" from this narrative, along with a link to "Learn more" about this creative process. The teaser text is retrieved from the project-level metadata. Depending upon the height of the image displayed on a particular preview page and the length of the teaser text, the preview page may automatically resize to accommodate the display of the teaser text. If a user follows the link to "Learn more," they are linked to that project's landing page, which displays the full creative text narrative. If the user closes the teaser text display, the preview page will automatically resize as needed.

RESPONSIVE DESIGN

The Digital Museum website is built using LGv2 and therefore responsive by design. We crafted our responsive behaviors to work well at any screen width, as opposed to designing around specific page width "break points." Inasmuch as the Digital Museum is an online presentation of a visual arts collection, we are also working on making the website as accessible as possible.

The homepage incorporates two examples of Wexler's art when viewed on a wide screen. On narrower screens, only one work is shown. The website title heading and navigation display is completely repurposed on the homepage. For streamlined maintenance, even though the visual design of the homepage is different than the design of the other pages on the site, the homepage uses the same LGv2 template as the rest of the website (e.g., it is in the same LGv2 group). The header and footer, including the title heading and site navigation, use the same HTML markup as the rest of the site but are styled to display differently. The size and verbosity of title heading text is optimized for best display and usability at different screen widths. Comparative examples are shown in figures 7.4, 7.5, and 7.6.

Figure 7.4. The Peter Wexler Digital Museum at Furman University homepage display on wide screen (this figure uses non-project images for demonstration purposes). *Images of website created by Kathie Sloan and copyright © 2015 Furman University. All rights reserved*

Figure 7.5. *The Peter Wexler Digital Museum* **at Furman University homepage display on medium screen (this figure uses a non-project image for demonstration purposes).** *Images of website created by Kathie Sloan and copyright © 2015 Furman University.* **All rights reserved**

The About webpage uses semantic HTML markup with properly nested headings and lists. The embedded video is sensibly positioned and sized, depending upon screen width. The project listing page, project landing pages, and project preview pages are also designed to optimally display their content at different screen widths. Within the constraints of the visual design, we attempted to make webpage controls usable via mouse and touch interfaces and on different-sized devices.

TRACKING USAGE WITH GOOGLE ANALYTICS

Assessment is an often neglected aspect of any project, and we were determined to build automated data collection into the Digital Museum from the beginning. We

Furman University

Figure 7.6.   The Peter Wexler Digital Museum at Furman University homepage display on narrow screen (this figure uses a non-project image for demonstration purposes). *Images of website created by Kathie Sloan and copyright © 2015 Furman University. All rights reserved*

Unless otherwise stated, all art images and concepts in the Digital Museum are the property of and copyright Peter Wexler. Digital image rights are held by Furman University, Greenville, SC. All rights reserved. View **Usage Guidelines.**

incorporated custom event trackers into the site's JavaScript files to do this. The user interactions that we track include use of the site navigation links, use of the item and project links to CONTENTdm, "depth" of page views in the project previews, and search query text. We plan to use this data, as part of broader assessment activities, to improve the website experience for our users.

CONCLUSION

We were presented with a unique and challenging opportunity to partner with an artist in the digitization of his life's work. We faced many challenges including the sheer volume of artwork, the novelty of digitizing and describing uncommon formats, and the adaptation of technologies to match our available time and expertise. Among our goals for the Peter Wexler Digital Museum at Furman University, we hoped to create an engaging website reminiscent of an art gallery with a simple and uncluttered user interface. We combined "generic" data-driven web development techniques with the capabilities of the newly released LGv2 in the process of accomplishing this goal. We took advantage of LibGuides' flexible design capabilities, Bootstrap, and jQuery to create a truly unique website with purpose-designed functionality.

ACKNOWLEDGMENT

The authors gratefully acknowledge the assistance of Kathie Sloan, Furman University Library digital projects specialist, in creating website image facsimiles for use with this chapter.

REFERENCE

FurmanUnivLibraries. April 2014. "Peter Wexler Digital Museum at Furman University." YouTube. www.youtube.com/watch?v=QvhelinnWy4.

8

Exhibition LibGuides
as Outreach Tools

Jennifer Schnabel, The Ohio State University
Brigitte Billeaudeaux, University of Memphis
Cody Behles, University of Memphis

Academic libraries often curate physical displays of collections materials as a way to engage and educate patrons (Fouracre 2015). In recent years, digitalization and web-based technologies have afforded librarians opportunities to reinvent how they make special collections available to a wider audience. We must continually assess user expectations and improve online discoverability in order to adequately display and describe digital materials (Severson 2015). Details about displays are now connected to our websites (Aloi et al. 2008), and quick response (QR) codes can efficiently link smart-phone users to online videos, podcasts, and the library catalog (Baker 2010). Libraries have long used online exhibitions as another way to promote collections online (Schnell 1996), and some librarians currently experiment with collaborative tools to encourage interactivity (Ress 2015). However, not all academic libraries have the time or resources to build online exhibitions, scan materials, manage content on multiple web and social media pages, and research new ways of improving online discoverability, while also carefully planning and executing exhibitions in their physical spaces. LibGuides provide the seamless solution to build, manage, and promote curated material in a single platform.

PURPOSE OF EXHIBITION LIBGUIDES

More than 1,500 academic libraries already use LibGuides to connect patrons to a variety of resources, research help, and relevant web links (Springshare, Inc. 2010). It therefore makes sense for librarians to also use the platform as an online extension of physical displays and exhibitions. LibGuides are familiar to librarians and patrons, are quick and easy to construct, and allow for multiple owners/editors to co-create while maintaining uniform style. Though LibGuides are sometimes used to promote a library's special collections department and holdings (Lewis and Griffin 2011), libraries can also create individual guides for each curated exhibition. Exhibition guides can maximize user engagement by serving several purposes.

SUGGESTED APPROACHES

Provide Contextual Information about Objects in the Cases

Even the largest academic libraries struggle with limited display spaces for exhibitions. Curators must find a balance between providing enough information about the objects and not overloading the visitor with too much text. A complementary LibGuide allows curators to provide additional background information like an encyclopedia entry, a government document, or a photograph. The guide can also include PDFs of complete documents that have been excerpted for the physical display. Traditionally, URLs are used to access websites via computers, tablets, and mobile devices. However, other tools, such as QR code readers, allow users to scan symbols—instead of typing—that will automatically connect them to websites. This includes LibGuides.

Connect Users to Additional Resources about the Topic

A customized guide offers patrons suggestions for further research. This includes articles, books, web sources, and collections from other institutions. The "Book from Catalog" feature can help direct patrons to relevant titles in the circulating collection. There is also an opportunity to cross-reference with the library's related subject or course guides using the "Guide List" feature, as well as provide ready-made boxes or widgets that subject librarians can copy into existing guides.

Highlight the Libraries' Born-Digital and Digitized Collections

For libraries acquiring born-digital materials, such as photographs or recordings, curators can use LibGuides as a way to incorporate these holdings into their physical exhibitions. Some institutions have the capacity to include audio and video components in their displays while others do not. In either environment, LibGuides offer patrons the opportunity to access selected born-digital or digitally formatted materials from off-site or post-exhibition.

Offer Opportunities to Cross-Promote Collections with Other Institutions

Library exhibitions often reflect current happenings, address social issues, or commemorate anniversaries of regional or national events. LibGuides can link library patrons to museums, historical societies, and other cultural organizations that are focused on similar themes by including social media feeds, using a common hashtag, or adding links to complementary programming. Hashtags and RSS feeds are tools born out of Web 2.0/the social web. Hashtags, rendered as "#" by computers, are popular tags that are utilized in different Web 2.0 environments. They have been popularized by social media sites such as Flickr, Twitter, Facebook, and Instagram and allow users to create searchable keywords that are attached to user-created content. These natural language tags help link content by pulling together everything created using the same hashtag. RSS feeds are systems that notify web users anytime a website to which they are subscribed is changed or updated. Hashtags and RSS feeds allow LibGuides users to quickly locate current events or discussions relating to their topic. This partnered approach to building exhibition LibGuides increases collection visibility.

Engage the Off-Campus Community

Not all community members can visit academic libraries due to accessibility issues. However, anyone with a computer and Internet connection can explore an exhibition LibGuide and learn about the topics and the collections used to illustrate the chosen theme. Links to nonproprietary resources allow those unaffiliated with the institution to access reliable information from home. Further, instructions on how to use the guest computers, if available in the library, may encourage further exploration if an interested community member wishes to visit.

Link Patrons to Online Research Help

Subject and course guides include contact information for the specialist who created them. Exhibition LibGuides provide the patron with an online forum to ask specific questions about the displays or request reference assistance pertaining to the topic. Chat widgets, e-mail links, and phone numbers can be embedded into guides and act as direct links to department personnel.

Inspire Teaching Faculty to Create Assignments

Instruction librarians and subject specialists can use exhibition LibGuides as a springboard to encourage their departments to create custom assignments. Examples may include a scavenger hunt, a response paper, or using the sources featured on the LibGuide. In some cases, corresponding course projects can inform the layout and content of the exhibition and supplemental guide. This idea will be addressed, in more detail, later in this chapter.

Invite Researchers to Explore the Collections

Online finding aids help a researcher investigate a collection's item list before deciding if he or she needs to visit the library in person. However, comprehensive exhibition LibGuides can inform scholars about related materials that may not appear in an expected collection. Special collections staff can also refer researchers to the guides in order to assist with inquiries.

Document the Physical Exhibition

After the physical displays are disassembled and the collections are returned to their secure homes, the LibGuide serves as a record of the exhibition that users can easily retrieve from the library's website. Embedded photographs and video recordings of the curated displays, as well as corresponding events, can add to the virtual experience of the online visitor unable to attend in person. LibGuides version 2 (LGv2) offers creators the option of choosing "Gallery Boxes" to highlight images in a slideshow format.

ADDITIONAL WAYS TO USE EXHIBITION LIBGUIDES

Exhibition LibGuides serve several purposes within the library in addition to user engagement. They allow librarians across branches and departments to collaborate. The exhibition and guide will often include materials from several areas of the library. This includes government documents, music, and maps—these may require the expertise of more than one person. By enlisting the help of colleagues, the exhibition curator or community engagement librarian does not have to build the guide alone. Each member of the team can take ownership of a section or topic. These guides, unlike those created for a course or one subject, are by nature more image-based and can showcase the staff's creativity in overall design. Student workers and graduate assistants can also take ownership of exhibition LibGuides. Doing so empowers them to engage in a meaningful library project they may include on their resumes.

PRESERVATION OPTIONS FOR LIBGUIDES

While the development and maintenance of a LibGuide during the event are essential to the success of any special collections exhibition, there is an aspect of stewardship after the life of the event that presents a challenge to librarians. The physical displays will eventually be replaced, but the digital counterparts have the potential to be maintained for future reference. Targeted curation, for a particular audience, shows there is a conscious attempt in exhibition development to elicit certain responses from viewers (Gurian 1991). The incorporation of multimedia types helps to develop these responses. In the case of special collections exhibitions that utilize LibGuides to provide context to a collection, the question of guide value outside of the context of its initial event is legitimate.

It should also be noted that the strategies for LibGuide preservation change based on the function it serves. A guide that is made in reference to a specific event, such as a special collections exhibition, varies considerably from the strategies employed for the preservation of a digital collection that is designed to host its own content as well as the guide with associated materials. These online exhibitions, which utilize a database to house both the content and its interpretation, are self-perpetuating. Museums and libraries often utilize these resources in conjunction with exhibitions. This method provides a fully encapsulated and preservable representation of the exhibition that is not dependent on the physical displays for context. Several free software programs exist to enable this process, including Collective Access, CollectionSpace, Omeka, Open Exhibits, and Pachyderm. However, LibGuides are better suited to include the ancillary materials that often accompany an exhibition in an academic library.

LibGuides preservation, as an exhibition aid, adds considerable value to the content of the exhibition for which it was created. It provides a curatorial vantage point while also contextualizing the collection contents for users. Although you could approach the preservation of LibGuides from several angles, depending on your skill level, we will outline two primary technical methods to accomplish this. The first is directly exporting data associated with the guide. This feature requires knowledge of Extensible Markup Language (XML). The second method facilitates robust preservation by utilizing HTML backup, or web-based encoded backup, of the content.

Preservation Method One

The raw XML data associated with a guide can be utilized in applications and future developments that will ensure your work is preserved after the exhibition finishes. This method provides a snapshot of the guide at a moment in time. It preserves the data and organization in a more limited way. The XML data is the raw code for a webpage. When this code is preserved and placed into a new web environment, it will re-create or duplicate the content of the page as it originally appeared when it was last saved. This makes XML data compatible with multiple operating systems and hardware types. Because of the cross-platform compatibility of XML documents, you are able to develop your guide content for future use. The XML data will ensure that the content does not deteriorate due to changes in technical requirements. You must be an administrator to extract XML data from a guide.

In LGv2, select Tools and Data Exports. Once selected, choose "Request Export" and "XML: Public Content." This will export all of the publicly visible content from your guides. If you wish to only export the content of a single guide into an XML file, you can select "Request XML Export" from within that guide.

Once you have created your XML file, it contains the data from your guides based on the box IDs used in the guide. This system allows you to easily navigate through the data and harvest content as needed. The information includes any script data so as to preserve the style of the content. XML data also preserves the metadata information. Therefore, future users will be able to see when content was added or changed and by whom. This more technical method of preservation provides a more robust archiving opportunity.

Preservation Method Two

Preservation using XML is the technical solution. However, a less technical option is directly exporting HTML content from the guide. Simply select "Create HTML Backup" from the upper right corner of the screen. Once you have done this and downloaded the file, you will be prompted to save a file with the guide ID included in the file name. This HTML file will preserve the look and feel of the guide, as well as maintaining any links that were included. This method, although simpler, is more likely to deteriorate over time as external links become inoperable, HTML styles are deprecated, and style sheets proprietary to Springshare are altered. All external links would need to be archived in order to truly preserve the complete look and feel of the guide. This includes scripts and the stylesheet languages like CSS. The HTML export does include Dublin Core metadata in the heading. This can be valuable as libraries attempt to index the resources they create. Archiving library-generated content is an essential part of the preservation model. Increasing prevalence of digital assets in special collections and exhibitions requires an aggressive archiving strategy to capture these resources.

EXHIBITION LIBGUIDES AT THE UNIVERSITY OF MEMPHIS

At the University of Memphis Libraries, special collections and outreach staff create LibGuides to support regularly scheduled exhibitions of special collections materials. Each exhibition is accompanied by a custom guide that includes specific topical resources like books, articles, manuscripts, and ephemera available in the collections. The guides also link to relevant and contextual information sources that can be accessed from community institutions and on the web. The guide serves as an online component to our three-case exhibition and allows the curators, usually a librarian and a special collections staff member, an additional space to include information that may not fit logistically in a physical display. All of these aspects come together in the LibGuide to provide a rich and meaningful experience for the user. Further, it is contextualized whether they are ever able to see the physical exhibition in person or not (Lewis and Griffin 2011).

Our exhibition LibGuide requires materials from all departments of the University of Memphis Libraries. Guides include links to books/e-books in the library's catalog, along with items and links to content from the library's special collections and government publications. In addition, special collections staff add bonus content on the LibGuide that is not included in the physical exhibition, like an audio recording or the verso of a painting. Along with in-house content, the exhibition team staff works to include local, regional, and national resources that can further enhance the content of guides. This includes anything from links to state and national parks that align with content from the guide, to museums and other cultural organizations that hold collections related to the exhibition's theme.

The University of Memphis Libraries began using LibGuides for special projects when the institution was awarded the *Bridging Cultures: Muslim Journeys Bookshelf* from the American Library Association (ALA) and the National Endowment for the Humanities (NEH) in 2012. The guide (libguides.memphis.edu/muslimjourneys) highlighted the library's display of twenty-five books as well as promoted the accompanying programs planned by several partner institutions: Christian Brothers University, the Memphis Public Library and Information Center, Muslims in Memphis, the Pakistani Association of Memphis, and the Memphis Student Association. The University of Memphis Libraries also created guides for other library and campus programs, such as Tiger Blue Goes Green (libguides.memphis.edu/TBGG2015), the university's annual sustainability initiative. The practice grew to include exhibition guides for curated physical displays in the Ned R. McWherter Library.

In 2013, the libraries participated in a Memphis-wide event to celebrate the centennial of local artist Carol Cloar's birth. The Preservation and Special Collections Department houses a manuscript collection that includes primary source materials of the artist's paintings along with materials documenting the artist's early works and travels. An exhibition was created for *Early and Rare: Selections from the Carroll and Pat Cloar Collection*, and the staff encountered the common issue of trying to select materials from a rich, unique collection to fit into limited display spaces: one window outside of the Special Collections Department and two freestanding cases in the first-floor rotunda. The LibGuides option presented a simple solution to our space problem.

The guide for *Early and Rare* (libguides.memphis.edu/summerofcloar), shown in figure 8.1, features biographical content related to the artist's early education and career, a page dedicated to current events happening around Memphis celebrating the artist's life and work, and bonus media content from the collection.

In addition, the guide gave the libraries an opportunity to cross-promote *Early and Rare* with area institutions like the Art Museum of the University of Memphis, the Brooks Museum of Art, and the David Lusk Gallery that were also hosting Carroll Cloar events and exhibitions. Together, representatives from the participating museums and libraries created a social media hashtag, #SummerofCloar, as a way to link posts about programming. The *Early and Rare* guide included an RSS feed, shown in figure 8.2, which displayed tweets relating to the joint initiative.

The success of both the exhibition and the guide inspired the libraries' staff to regularly use LibGuides as extensions of the physical displays that staff presented throughout the year. Many of the University of Memphis Libraries' exhibitions have been curated in connection with events and celebrations happening on campus and in the community. *Woven into Words: Tennessee Women Making History* (libguides.

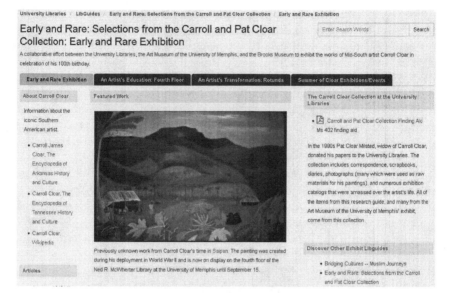

Figure 8.1. Landing page of the exhibition LibGuide that accompanies *Early and Rare: Selections from the Pat and Carroll Cloar Collection.*

Figure 8.2. RSS feed of tweets that included the hashtag "#SummerofCloar."

memphis.edu/TNWomen) was inspired by Women's History Month 2015 and included a partnership with an online history course to build a digital project with primary resources. The accompanying LibGuide included links to all campus events for the month. In turn, the guide served as the libraries' primary link on the university's Women's History Month website. Users could visit the guide and explore the rich resources around the highlighted themes. Other exhibitions and guides have been integral and informative components of the University of Memphis's annual Veterans Day events (libguides.memphis.edu/VeteransDay), the fiftieth anniversary of the Civil Right Act of 1964 (libguides.memphis.edu/civilrightsact1964), and the annual Delta symposium (libguides.memphis.edu/mississippi_delta).

LibGuides give creators many options when it comes to site building. According to Leibiger and Aldrich (2013), LibGuides support a social creator model that can help alleviate the time burden on staff by allowing borrowing, copying, and mapping from other guides. Whole pages, content boxes, and page links can be shared, which cuts down on the time required to create the shell, and in some cases the content, while also freeing up more time for filling the guide with subject-relevant materials. Staff members should not reinvent the wheel when formatting the guide. Copying features from other guides is a benefit that helps build in extra time for creation at institutions that lack a full-time, dedicated exhibitions staff.

New features in LGv2, like boxes that span the entire page in the tabbed navigation view, allow for themed introductory image headers to be added to pages. This helps create a cohesive visual impact that lets users know that content related to a specific topic, like World War II, will be the focus (Springshare, Inc. 2015). Our library exhibitions team began using more elaborate headers as visual markers to make each guide feel more a part of the physical exhibition as opposed to a standard subject or course guide. The first exhibition to feature these headers was *From Active Duty to Veteran: Honoring Military Service in America* (LibGuides.memphis.edu/activedutytoveteran) in fall 2014.

LibGuides' easy-to-use content management system (CMS) allows for uniform design and responsive web delivery that lets users access content via mobile devices without sacrificing access to content or original formatting (Leibiger and Aldrich 2013). It also offers archives managers a venue for housing and displaying a collection's gems within the confines of limited space. LibGuides only accept images, text, and media that are 10MB and under. However, this should not be seen as a limitation—it is an opportunity.

The CMS features of LibGuides allow for archives managers to display content in such a way that it can used by patrons, but the quality is lower and does not allow the digital item to be a useful surrogate of the original outside of the context of the guide or the library's exhibition. Best practices for the creation of preservation surrogates far exceed permissible file sizes in the LibGuides environment. A preservation copy of an 8 x 11-inch image is eight times larger than the size available for singular content in the system. Images are saved together on the LibGuides server, and guide creators can maintain a personal collection of images and other media that can be shared among other creators or remain protected and not shared. This works well with features that allow for content boxes to have gallery displays and mixed-media types (Springshare, Inc. 2015).

A way to help organize and fill the guide is by creating a consistent layout. Always having physical books from the library's catalog displayed in the "Book from the Catalog" content box on the left side of a guide, while displaying the library's e-book resources on the right side of the guide, helps reduce the amount of time spent looking for that particular item. If sufficient resources are not available to follow this plan, it is best to fill content space with alternate but relevant information. One example, shown in figure 8.3, comes from our exhibition LibGuide for *Woven into Words: Tennessee Women Making History* (libguides.memphis.edu/TNWomen). The first two tabs have dedicated boxes for physical and electronic resources housed at the library. Other tabs use content boxes to highlight resources from special collections and government publications.

Figure 8.3. Landing page of the exhibition LibGuide that accompanies *Tennessee Women Making History*, **curated in support of Women's History Month 2015.**

More often than not, the staff finds more resources to include in a guide than they have time to gather and cull. Between content from library collections and relevant information that can be found on the web, the LibGuides fill up quickly. If not curated properly, they become cluttered and confusing, and they lose their impact as online ambassadors of the library's exhibition. Collaboration among exhibition staff helps streamline the selection process and the overall organization of the guide. This practice gives the staff a logistical upper hand when selecting content for the guide and facilitating any digital preservation that must occur throughout the exhibition.

Time and staff are the most important assets to consider when creating guides. The technology available in LibGuides has changed the way librarians provide information to patrons. Extensible content boxes and innovative, consistent design provide endless opportunities for staff to reach users while providing a meaningful experience.

DEVELOPMENT OF BEST PRACTICES

Early and Rare: Selections from the Carroll and Pat Cloar Collection was the libraries' first LibGuide to accompany a library exhibition, and the process set a standard for how to build future guides as online extensions of physical exhibitions to help achieve outreach goals. Many of these best practices are fluid since exhibition and display planning in libraries requires flexibility due to limited staff, time, and resources. The general rule for adding LibGuides to a library's exhibition program is to work smarter, not harder, by integrating the goals for the exhibition and the guide early on in the planning process. In addition, involving library or community stakeholders in discussions as soon as possible helps maximize LibGuides' usefulness to the targeted audience. There is no set formula for creating our exhibition guides—each will be a unique presentation of library collections and online resources. However, there are several elements that should be considered when building them.

Establish a Vision and Identify Your Audience

As the exhibition begins to take shape, keep in mind how LibGuides will complement the physical displays and best serve patrons. Curators can maximize their time in the collections by tagging potential "gems" for the guide throughout the research and gathering process for the exhibition. Keep in mind that although some items may not work well in physical display cases, they may add relevance and value to the theme and are worth considering for the online guide. Also, scanning items properly to display in the guide is time-consuming. But it allows preservation staff to fulfill departmental best practices, such as local storage protocols and file size guidelines, while creating digital masters in which LibGuides-quality files can be created. If these selections are made early, they will be available to the exhibition staff for inclusion in all possible promotional venues.

Initial conversations should also address how the online guide will best serve the intended audience by asking questions like: "How will the LibGuide act as an online extension of the exhibition?" or "Will the LibGuide cover topics that are not addressed in the physical displays?" An early organization plan for both components can also serve as a reference point if either the exhibition or guide begins to grow unwieldy. The organizers should choose topic areas judiciously so that the guide does not become too cluttered. Selecting four to six topic areas on which to focus will look much cleaner than having fifteen different tabs stacked up on the guide. Finally, it is helpful to have a plan for promoting the exhibition before designing the guide. Consider which images will appear on the posters, bookmarks, calendar listings, and social media headings. The LibGuide should reflect the exhibition design as well as coordinate with the look of promotional materials.

Build Your Team

Invite appropriate colleagues once you have created a vision and identified an audience for the exhibition guide. No more than five or six people should be needed to help with design and final content choices. Consider the size of the exhibition staff and the ways you can best utilize their work time. What are some of the topic areas that will be covered in the guide? Are there others who could contribute specialized knowledge or skills? Think of including those who may not normally participate in exhibitions or outreach but who would bring a specific skill set to the group. For instance, do you know a staff member with excellent design skills, a student worker interested in the exhibition theme, or a graduate assistant in library school? If colleagues are unaccustomed to working with LibGuides, another team member can conduct a quick training session. When constructing a more comprehensive guide, consider assigning each team member a topic page. One person from the exhibition staff should coordinate the effort to ensure the guide is consistent with the themes of the physical displays.

Discuss Design and Layout

One of the first selections when creating a guide is navigation type. Tabbed navigation guides work well for exhibitions. They allow for the use of columns and can present a lot of information at once in an organized manner. Side navigation is more appropriate for guides with lots of topic areas. The benefit of side navigation is that pages have more real estate to focus on one topic with the ability to create subpages that can provide additional space as needed.

Libraries may not have dedicated staff to create physical displays and accompanying guides. People may rotate on and off of an exhibition team or committee, and planning and execution must fit into the schedules of their primary duties. Therefore, it is vital to employ time-saving measures while not sacrificing the quality of the final product. Since the LibGuides platform allows for sharing content and layout, consider copying boxes, widgets, or entire pages from existing guides and customizing them if necessary. Use the LibGuides "Guide Lists" as well as the selected boxes of the exhibition guide to include links to related subject or course guides and other online resources that may be of interest.

If this is not the libraries' first exhibition LibGuide, revisit previous work and see if some of the same elements can be used in the current exhibition guide. The LibGuides "Reuse Existing Box" tool enables one to either copy the content or map to the original box. By checking "copy," an exact copy of the content and code in the original box is created, but creators can make changes as needed. The default setting maps to the original box, which means that all changes to the original will be reflected in the mapped version.

Look for Opportunities for Partnerships and Cross-Promotion

Does your display or exhibition complement a larger campus or community initiative? Contact academic departments, cultural institutions, or municipal offices to discuss ways you can link to webpages, social media accounts, or online resources to cross-promote related lectures and programs. Consider creating common hashtags for social media platforms, and encourage your patrons to post on their accounts after they visit the exhibition or explore the guide. Members and visitors of partner institutions can do the same.

Collaborate with special collections staff to digitize items that were selected for inclusion in the guide. The digitization workflow for preservation purposes takes more time than creating a digital surrogate for the guide. It is tempting to quickly scan an item and post the file online. However, a preservation-quality surrogate should be created first and then a much lower-quality surrogate can be created from the preservation-quality copy. This strategy reduces potential damage to the original item and creates a preservation master from which additional copies can be made in the future.

Use QR Codes and Friendly URLs

Exhibition guides help create a presence on the web for physical displays, but it is not always easy to encourage people to use and share them. Knowing where, how, and when to promote your exhibition is helpful. In addition to hashtags, there are several methods to get the word out about the exhibition guide. Quick response (QR) codes allow direct online access from physical displays, exhibition posters, and all other promotional materials. In addition to QR codes, use the "Add/Edit Friendly URL" feature to generate a short URL for the LibGuide on displays and marketing materials for patrons who don't have mobile devices with QR readers.

Highlight More Than Your Physical Collections

As Lewis and Griffin noted, "While a LibGuide does not take the place of a digital repository or provide out-of-the-box functionality for presenting large digital collections, it does afford the means for creating the front end of a contextualized web presentation" (2011, 6). Exhibition guides provide another way for libraries to present their digital collections. Also, look for opportunities to connect patrons to already digitized materials that live elsewhere on the web, like those images and documents available as part of the Library of Congress American Memory Project (memory.loc.gov/ammem/index.html).

CONCLUSION

The LibGuides platform is great for extending and promoting physical exhibitions in an online environment. Patrons can access contextual information, view bonus archival material, and link to relevant websites and digital collections in order to experience richer exhibition engagement. Librarians can use the exhibition guide as a way to collaborate across departments and empower staff members and student workers to participate in a meaningful library project. Even with limited staff time, thoughtful planning and teamwork can make the process of creating an exhibition guide manageable and enjoyable. Finally, preservation options enable libraries to capture images, text, and links for later access. Exhibition LibGuides can continue to engage patrons and inspire research long after the physical displays are dismantled.

ACKNOWLEDGMENTS

The authors would like to thank Cindi Nichols, Betsy Eckert, Zach Sandberg, Anna Swearengen, Blake Galbreath, and Jim Cole for their work on exhibition LibGuides at the University of Memphis.

REFERENCES

Aloi, Michael, Lisa Esposito, Joyce Gotsch, Diane Holliday, and Chris Kretz. 2008. "Technology of Displays." *Technical Services Quarterly 24*(4): 15–27.

Baker, Laura. 2010. "Making Physical Objects Clickable: Using Mobile Tags to Enhance Library Displays." *Journal of Library Innovation 1*(2).

Fouracre, Dorothy. 2015. "Making an Exhibition of Ourselves? Academic Libraries and Exhibitions Today." *Journal of Academic Librarianship 41*(4).

Gurian, Elaine. 1991. "Noodling Around with Exhibition Opportunities." In *Exhibiting Cultures: The Poetics and Politics of Museum Display,* edited by Ivan Karp and Steven Lavine, 176–90. Washington, DC: Smithsonian Institution Press.

Leibiger, Carol A., and Alan W. Aldrich. 2013. "'The Mother of All LibGuides': Applying Principles of Communication and Network Theory in LibGuide Design from Pathfinders to LibGuides." Paper presented at Association of College and Research Libraries, Indianapolis, Indiana, April 10–13.

Lewis, Barbara, and Melanie Griffin. 2011. "Special Collections and the New Web: Using Libguides to Provide Meaningful Access." *Journal of Electronic Resources Librarianship 23*(1): 20–29.

Ress, Sunghae. 2015. "Special Collections: Improving Access and Usability." *The Reference Librarian 56*(1): 52–58.

Schnell, Eric H. 1996. "The World Wide Web." *Internet Reference Services Quarterly 1*(4): 33–41.

Severson, Richard James. 2015. *The Principles of Information Ethics.* Routledge: New York.

Springshare, Inc. 2010. "Clients." www.springshare.com/libguides/clients.html.

———. 2015. "Migrating to LibGuides v2 (and Going Live!)." help.springshare.com/libguides/migration.

IV

DATA-DRIVEN
DECISION MAKING

9

Maximizing LibAnswers Data to Drive Workflow Processes

Andrea Hebert, Louisiana State University
Alice L. Daugherty, Louisiana State University
David Dunaway, Louisiana State University

Louisiana State University (LSU) is a designated land-, sea-, and space-grant research center that serves as the flagship university in the state of Louisiana. Located in Baton Rouge, LSU enrolls more than thirty thousand students and employs 1,300 faculty teaching and researching within the sciences, engineering, social sciences, humanities, arts, veterinary medicine, and law. The LSU Libraries include Middleton Library, which houses the main collection and serves the entire campus and local community, while special collections reside at Hill Memorial Library. The Veterinary Medicine Library and Law Center Library are administratively separate from LSU Libraries. In addition to the main collection and its associated circulation and reference service points, Middleton Library has two additional distinct collections and service points: Music Resources and Government Documents.

The majority of student touchpoints occur via the main reference service point research desk located in the Reference and Instruction Services (RIS) Department. The LSU Libraries had a complete overhaul of administration in 2014, and at that time the RIS Department staff advocated for, and secured the procurement of, Springshare products. This change in library administration opened new avenues for restructuring workflows and included a much-needed administrative emphasis on properly recording and reporting library metrics.

Initially, the RIS Department trialed and purchased LibAnswers to manage e-mail and chat reference as well as a searchable knowledge bank available on our website. Subsequently, staff members within RIS quickly realized the functions within LibAnswers would be advantageous to the assessment and capture of statistics for all reference service points and therefore worked with the assessment librarian to build a streamlined approach for improving data collection accuracy.

LIBANSWERS AND ITS COMPONENTS

LibAnswers is a versatile product that can manage virtual reference (VR), create a searchable frequently asked questions (FAQ) database, record reference statistics, and analyze data collected with the product. LibAnswers has several components: Dashboard, Answers, LibChat, RefAnalytics, and Status Management. Libraries can choose to use as many or as few of the components as their organization needs.

When the LSU Libraries first obtained access to LibAnswers, the system defaults were generic. One of the RIS librarians serving as a LibAnswers administrator customized it for us by modifying the system settings. A system name (Ask Us!) was assigned, and institution information was entered (e.g., administrator e-mail address, the library's URL, the university name, as well as the support e-mail address and time zone). Springshare offers custom URLs for a fee, so the libraries' ITS department created the URL askus.lib.lsu.edu, and Springshare assigned it to our LibAnswers site. Entering the LibAnswers URL into a web browser takes you to our homepage. We set up this up to reflect the libraries' parent website by customizing colors, headers, and footers. Libraries can customize these features by inserting JavaScript or Cascading Style Sheet (CSS) information under "Look & Feel" in System Settings.

Dashboard

The Dashboard gives an overview of what is currently active in the system and serves as a jumping-off point for the product's other features. There is also an area for administrative announcements for sharing updates or instructions with users.

Answers

Answers handles patron-submitted questions. These questions are called tickets. Patrons can submit tickets through e-mail, embedded widgets, Twitter, or short message service (SMS). Springshare can supply the SMS number. Staff at the Research Desk can answer incoming tickets, or if a question requires specialized knowledge, they can assign the ticket to a staff member with relevant knowledge or expertise. FAQs can also be created in Answers. FAQ entries are added to a searchable knowledge base that can be internal or public-facing.

LibChat

LibChat is the real-time messaging component of LibAnswers that is set up under the Admin tab. Librarians can attach files and transfer synchronous chats to other librarians logged into the system. Unresolved or unanswered chats can be converted into tickets and then assigned to a particular staff member who replies asynchronously. LibChat records transcripts and time-stamps chats interactions. It also allows for the creation of canned messages. LibAnswers allows creation of various chat widgets for different webpages. The administrator can use the in-page chat setup, with a permanently embedded chat widget displayed in a box on the homepage, or create an in-page button that will open a pop-out widget chat box as well as a side-out tab that will float on the left, right, or bottom of the page. The chat boxes or tabs can be displayed wherever patrons may need help on the website.

RefAnalytics

RefAnalytics records statistics. This component is highly customizable to the type of statistics a library wishes to collect, and the granularity is determined by the needs of the library or service point. RefAnalytics is set up under the Admin tab and can be used to manage both desk and VR statistics. Statistics are date- and time-stamped, which allows library managers to identify times of peak usage. Libraries have five analytics datasets by default but can obtain more from Springshare by increasing their subscription allowance. Datasets are customizable, and Springshare also offers a Reference Effort Assessment Data (READ) Scale template as an option.

Stats

Stats allows users to view data concerning system statistics collected via LibAnswers. Statistics are broken down by general statistics, statistics about tickets, SMS questions, and FAQ questions. A Query Spy feature allows library staff to view questions that were not fully submitted. Query Spy works by capturing text users type into query boxes but do not submit. Reviewing these queries can help libraries identify which LibGuides or library webpages may need revision.

Status Management

Status Management helps the library communicate about the status of systems and allows patrons to give the library feedback or ideas about services—similar to a suggestion box.

BEHIND THE SCENES AT LSU LIBRARIES

In fall 2014, with new library administration in place, the assessment librarian was tasked with reporting all American Research Libraries (ARL) statistics, a project previously handled by the dean of LSU Libraries. Without a written record or any institutional knowledge of how different metrics were tracked or recorded for formal reporting purposes, the assessment librarian had to piece together past practices and then formulate and implement entirely new systems for gathering reportable data.

During this period, a new department head was appointed to LSU Libraries' RIS, which is responsible for the largest number of reference transactions. A member of the RIS team discovered that reference statistics had been incorrectly reported in prior years. This discrepancy added another layer of complexity to the task of reporting reliable statistics. Unfortunately, prior statistics included directional questions, such as "Where is the tutorial center?" and the ARL directions specifically stated:

> EXCLUDE SIMPLE DIRECTIONAL QUESTIONS. A directional transaction is an information contact that facilitates the logistical use of the library and that does not involve the knowledge, use, recommendations, interpretation, or instruction in the use or creation of information sources other than those that describe the library, such as schedules, floor plans, and handbooks. (Association of Research Libraries 2014, 7)

Concurrent with the assessment librarian's experiences, the RIS Department had trialed and purchased different pieces of the Springshare suite of products, one of which was LibAnswers. Although the RIS Department originally adopted LibAnswers to consolidate its VR services, its other functions became central to LSU Libraries' use of the product. Before the introduction of LibAnswers, the RIS department collected ARL statistics using a simple homegrown Access database to take a weekly sample three times per year. The Access database had three levels of librarian-patron interaction: information/check-out/fix, reference, and research strategies.

Information/check-out/fix questions referred to questions that did not use professional knowledge or consultation of reference sources. Reference questions were defined as those that required professional knowledge or reference source consultation. Research strategy questions included any reference question that required constructing a detailed research strategy. The database also required librarians to identify each interaction as in person, phone, or VR. Each entry was time-stamped.

Although the homegrown system allowed librarians at the Research Desk to include VR statistics, only chat questions could be recorded. E-mail questions were tracked in a different homegrown Access database and were added to the count manually. There was no data about the date and time for the submission and answering of e-mail questions. In addition, SMS questions came in through Google Voice and had to be added to the final tally. Data had to be exported from the Access database and manipulated with Excel to identify reference trends. Visualizing data required the use of pivot tables to create charts. Pivot tables allow users to target specific intersections of large datasets for analysis. There was no quick, on-the-fly method for interpreting the data.

The RIS Department decided to try using the RefAnalytics component in LibAnswers to collect statistics after the regular fall sampling of questions was completed. The module was set up to reflect the form used in our Access database. We recorded how the question was submitted (e.g., VR, phone, in person) and the type of question asked (e.g., info/check-out/fix, reference, research strategies). LibAnswers applied time-stamps to each statistics entry just as our Access database had done.

RefAnalytics provided a better user experience than our in-house solution. The librarians and graduate assistants working at the Research Desk found no significant difference in the recording procedures. However, they did find having one central location and login for VR and desk statistics to be advantageous. In addition, the visualization tools were a vast improvement over manipulating data in Excel. The system automatically tracked e-mail questions and eliminated the additional step of compiling that data and then including it in the final reference statistics. Streamlined recording and the increased ability to identify service trends led the RIS Department to take daily statistics, as a pilot, to understand Research Desk traffic patterns.

Gaining Buy-In and Support from Library Administration

A small group of LibAnswers administrators—two RIS librarians, the new RIS Department head, and the assessment librarian—met to discuss how best to implement the system. They focused on specific reporting parameters that would buffer inaccuracies while providing levels of description that allowed easy question analysis. Ideally, this new system would provide a proper count of lower-effort transactions (e.g., directional questions, printing questions).

Additionally, the RIS head wanted to use the built-in Reference Effort Assessment Data (READ) Scale template as a measurement tool and LibAnswers as a collection solution. The READ Scale

> is a six-point scale tool for recording vital supplemental qualitative statistics gathered when reference librarians assist users with their inquiries or research-related activities by placing an emphasis on recording the skills, knowledge, techniques and tools utilized by the librarian during a reference transaction. (Gerlich and Berard 2007, 7)

After the administrative team evaluated the usefulness and fit of the product within our current workflow, the assessment librarian met with the newly appointed associate dean of Public Services to discuss this possibility. She proposed launching LibAnswers with the READ Scale option implemented across all reference service points in the libraries. This included the reference desks in Music Resources, Government Documents, and Special Collections.

The administrative team decided to simplify the parameters of the RIS tracking method by moving away from submission type (e.g., VR, phone, in person) and question type (e.g., info/check-out/fix, reference, research strategy). This was because a large portion of inaccurate data reported to ARL included directional questions. The team decided the first scaffold in the new submission system would reflect whether the answer to the question fell into the category of "library" or "non-library" and the second tier would be the READ Scale rating. The definition of "library" for this purpose meant any use of a library resource or referral to a library service. The definition of "non-library" indicated any referral to a building or service not within the administrative control of the libraries—even if housed within the library building, for example, the Shell Tutorial Center located on the first floor of Middleton Library. The use of "library" and "non-library" categories combined with the READ Scale easily allows us to separate out directional questions not wanted by ARL. We do not count entries marked as "non-library" or "library" READ Scale 1 in final data reporting.

Launching at Service Desks

One of the more difficult challenges faced during our rollout of LibAnswers and the READ Scale was instilling the habit of recording data for every transaction. Our legacy practice had been to record three separate samples of one week's statistics and then use a formula to project a twelve-month total. Our formula took the mean average of three sampled weeks and multiplied by thirty-four. This formula excluded summer months and holidays periods as they were deemed irrelevant.

The other reference service points within the libraries had different ideas for tracking their reference statistics. After separate meetings with the heads of Music Resources, Government Documents, and Special Collections, we found that each unit was working independently and without clear guidance as to what data to collect or report. Staff from each unit wanted clear directions and reasons for data collection. Unlike the RIS Department, these units had staff tracking transactions daily. They were also still using paper, pencil, and hash marks as their preferred method of data collection—and every service transaction was marked on paper whether it was reference or not.

The data from these units were never transferred to an electronic format. Therefore, no usable analysis was performed nor was any historical record kept for trend-line comparisons. We needed consistent and accurate data collection across the libraries. The introduction of LibAnswers and the READ Scale offered an opportunity to standardize terminology and data collection methods. It also gave us an opportunity to bring reporting into line with ARL's definitions.

REAL-WORLD BEST PRACTICES: LIBANSWERS DATA AND WORKFLOW PROCESSES AT LSU

Reference statistics in most academic libraries are declining, and LSU Libraries' experience is no exception (Kyrillidou 2012, 21). Before the implementation of LibAnswers with the READ Scale, the best data the assessment librarian could offer administration was a set of numbers with rudimentary definitions of the metrics they represented. We could determine blocks of time and the busiest day of the week at the main Research Desk. However, this used a small sample and was skewed by factors that affected library traffic (e.g., weather, campus, and community events). Using LibAnswers with the READ Scale to collect data on a daily basis goes beyond these rudimentary counts and provides a measure of professional effort or time spent per question. We now collect VR transcripts and statistics, desk statistics with READ Scale ratings, and customized service desk statistics (e.g., referrals and special collections exhibit visitors).

Internal Statistics for Departments

The level of customization that LibAnswers provides allows each service desk the opportunity to use different metrics important to their daily tasks. The LibAnswers administrator initially created datasets for the RIS desk, Special Collections, and Government Documents. All three locations used the READ Scale to collect reference transactions. The setup screen for datasets allows for activation of the READ Scale by selecting *yes* or *no* from a drop-down menu.

In addition to the READ Scale, there are ten metadata fields that can be labeled, and each field can have up to thirty values entered. None of the datasets used by LSU Libraries contains more than three questions. This simplifies recording but also allows for the addition of questions if the need arises. For example, each of the libraries' datasets has a field labeled "Question Type" with two possible values: Library and Non-Library. This allows staff to track both questions about library services and general questions about the campus. The RIS dataset only includes this question and the READ Scale.

Other service desks customized the datasets to match their unique needs. For example, in addition to using the READ Scale, the Government Documents department records the type of task (e.g., assisting patrons with fiche and film reader or printers, assisting patrons by phone, and assisting patrons in person). They also track referrals to the circulation department, the main Research Desk, Special Collections, and nonspecified locations.

After installing and using LibAnswers at the reference desk within Special Collections, that department head requested a customized format for their Public Services desk to include not only the READ Scale but also their referrals to other units within Special Collections. They also wanted to track the number of visitors to the Special Collections' exhibit hall. After using the product for several months, the head of Special Collections is still unsure of its usefulness. This stems from a bimodal purpose in the collection of the data. The department head wants a tool that captures the unique services provided by Special Collections staff and provides performance evaluation data, whereas the assessment librarian's interests are in reporting transactions on a macro level.

Staffing Decisions

Data collected with LibAnswers is easily visualized. Users can view it in multiple ways that include tables, pie charts, column charts, and graphs. It allows users to select which statistics they want to view and then customize the period they want to examine by year, month, week, day, or hour. This is especially helpful when assessing librarians' efforts in answering research and public services questions. Using the READ Scale with LibAnswers means those who make staffing decisions can easily determine not only how many questions are being asked on specific days or at specific times but also the level of effort and knowledge needed to answer the questions. This information provides concrete evidence for managerial decisions related to staffing and program planning.

The data collected by RIS demonstrated the need to reorganize staffing models. Staff were spending a significant amount of professional time answering basic questions. We made the decision to cut back hours that the service desk was open based on this data—RIS moved from double staffing at the desk to single staffing except at peak hours. The low volume of library-related questions on Saturdays supported the decision to close the desk on Saturdays. These data-driven changes freed up significant time for RIS, up to eight hours per week, per librarian, in some cases. This extra time allowed librarians to concentrate on their liaison responsibilities and helped the department transition its focus to one-on-one consultations, outreach, and instructional touchpoints.

The VR transcripts and statistics combined with the RIS desk statistics also altered the RIS Department's practices. Traditionally, librarians and graduate students working at the Research Desk were responsible for answering all chat and e-mail questions submitted by library users. The head of RIS studied our VR statistics after dropping to single coverage at the RIS desk. The number of chat questions was low. She decided that librarians could log into LibChat at their desks. Staff members working at the Research Desk could still answer e-mail questions during downtimes or transfer them to the appropriate staff member.

CONCLUSION

LSU Libraries used the purchase and launch of LibAnswers as an opportunity to evaluate legacy methods of tracking and recording reference transaction metrics throughout the library system. Implementing LibAnswers with the READ Scale took approximately six months for all relevant service points after receiving administrative approval. LSU Libraries no longer relies on a small sample to report service statistics, and lower-level questions are categorized as such and excluded in reports to ARL.

Implementing the READ Scale using LibAnswers was a simple and effective way to standardize reference statistics collection over multiple library departments. The flexibility to provide all service desks customized tracking metrics, important to their daily tasks, eliminated hash marks and paper copies. This also consolidated data in a central location and provided tools to make data interpretation fast and easy while also giving individual department heads access to their own department's statistics. The flexibility of this product for input measures, and clean reporting of those measures, provides easy-to-access hard data for staffing and service decisions.

REFERENCES

Association of Research Libraries. 2014. "ARL Statistics Questionnaire, 2013–14, Instructions for Completing the Questionnaire." www.libqual.org/documents/admin/14instruct.pdf.

Gerlich, Bella Karla, and G. Lynn Berard. 2007. "Introducing the READ Scale: Qualitative Statistics for Academic Reference Services." *Georgia Library Quarterly* 43(4): 7–13. digitalcommons.kennesaw.edu/glq/vol43/iss4/4.

Kyrillidou, Martha. 2012. "Research Library Trends: A Historical Picture of Services, Resources, and Spending." *Research Library Issues* (280): 20–27. publications.arl.org/rli280/.

10

Pay Attention to the Data behind the Curtain

Leveraging LibGuides Analytics for Maximum Impact

Jamie L. Emery, MS, Saint Louis University
Sarah E. Fancher, MS, Saint Louis University

One of the notable advantages of LibGuides version 2 (LGv2) is the availability of enhanced statistics, which provide a variety of insights into LibGuides users' research needs and information-seeking behaviors. These insights inform guide curation and improve the usefulness and findability of an institution's LibGuides when analyzed thoughtfully. In this chapter we will discuss, using illustrative examples from our own institution's LibGuides statistics, the data available via LGv2 and how analysis of this data can and should inform site design and content. We recognize that librarians at many institutions may not be able to devote significant blocks of time to detailed data analysis; therefore we have summarized what we believe to be the most impactful and transferable best practices in the "Recommendations for Best Practices" section of the chapter.

Saint Louis University (SLU), a Catholic, Jesuit university located in St. Louis, Missouri, is a doctoral-degree granting institution with a total enrollment of 13,287 (Saint Louis University 2015). There are three campus libraries—the Vincent C. Immel Law Library, the Medical Center Library, and our flagship, Pius XII Memorial Library. Our LGv2 system (libguides.slu.edu) includes 378 guides, 247 of which are currently "published" and viewable by the public. Of these published guides, 131 are categorized as subject guides, 50 are course-specific guides, 54 are guides related to library collections and services, and 12 are practical "how to" guides.

We examined LibGuides statistics available to us as LibGuides CMS users who have migrated to LGv2. These were accessed via our Dashboard and include statistics related to the LibGuides homepage, guides, sessions, browser/OS data, searches, assets, and aggregate system content. LibGuides CMS is an upgrade to the base LibGuides package and includes several additional features, including the ability to organize guides into groups, customize the appearance of individual templates and guides, and access enhanced statistics. Specifically, session, search, and browser/OS statistics are available to LibGuides CMS users only. LibGuides CMS users also have access to information about referring websites for homepage, guide pages, and asset views. We do not subscribe to the optional LibGuides e-reserve module and therefore do not have accompanying e-reserves statistics via LibGuides. We primarily examined data from the fiscal year ending June 30, 2015, but examined comparative data from the previous year and succeeding months when necessary.

INSIGHTS AND OPPORTUNITIES FOR DATA-DRIVEN DECISION MAKING

Homepage Tracking

Homepage tracking statistics, available only to system administrators, provide information about daily or monthly views of the LibGuides system homepage (not the homepage of any particular guide). They also provide referrer URLs to the homepage for a given date range and the number of related referrals. When analyzing data from fiscal year 2015, we observed usage patterns that generally correlated with the academic year, as seen in figure 10.1. Homepage views were lowest in December (206 views) and the summer months and highest in September (2,806 views). This indicates that major site revisions would be best scheduled during December, June, or July, when they would be least disruptive to our users.

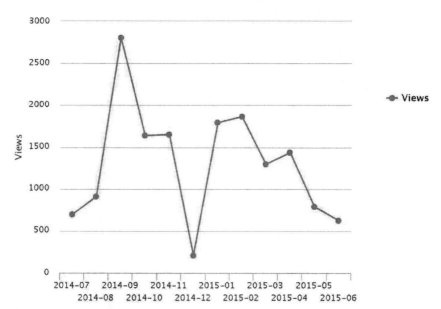

Figure 10.1. SLU LibGuides system homepage views by month during fiscal year ending June 30, 2015.

We closely analyzed homepage view statistics for the months before, during, and after the launches of new SLU campus library websites in fiscal year 2014–2015. These website launches were relevant in terms of LibGuides homepage views because two of the new sites provide users with access to LibGuides in different ways than their predecessors.

SLU's new Vincent C. Immel Law Library website launched on January 31, 2015, (law.slu.edu/library) and uses an embedded LibGuides widget to display only Law Library guides on the site, bypassing the SLU LibGuides system homepage and other guides entirely. Examination of our LibGuides homepage data showed that views did not decrease from the previous year after launching the new Law Library website. Yet we observed a large spike in the usage of our law guides following the launch of the new website. The Law Library's approach of using a LibGuides widget to display only law guides directly on their website has generated increased guide usage and is a model that our Medical Center Library is considering replicating in the future.

The SLU Libraries website (lib.slu.edu), which serves as the Pius XII Memorial Library website, debuted on May 15, 2015. The new website gives users the option to not only go to our LibGuides homepage and browse guides by subject, but also to bypass our LibGuides homepage and search our guides directly from the SLU Libraries website via a search widget. Our LibGuides homepage data showed that views did decrease slightly after the new SLU Libraries' website launch and were slow to rebound during fall 2015. In the future we'll need to continue to analyze LibGuides homepage views in conjunction with our overall site usage data in order to ascertain whether LibGuides use is being affected by the change in our access models via our new library websites.

Guide Tracking

Guide statistics, available to all regular-level users, provide information about the total number of views for a guide or collection of guides during a selected time period. Reports can be run on individual guides, groups of guides (e.g., a particular campus library's guides), or a particular user's own guides. Data may be viewed in daily or monthly increments and displayed for guides of all statuses or limited to published, unpublished, or private. We examined monthly views of our guides, regardless of status, for fiscal year 2014–2015 and identified our top ten most-used guides as well as our low-use guides. Guide usage is shown in table 10.1.

High-Use Guides

Course guides and program-specific subject guides that are frequently used in classroom instruction received high use. For example, our most-used guide was our Social Work guide, which is shared with all incoming master of social work students as part of a mandatory introduction to the SLU Libraries. Also heavily used was our ENGL 1500, 1900, and 1920: Freshman Writing Program guide that is regularly

Table 10.1. Top ten SLU LibGuides by usage during fiscal year ending June 30, 2015.

Guide	Total Views
Social Work Guide	9,725
EndNote Tips	8,151
Eastern Orthodoxy	3,532
ENGL 1500, 1900, and 1920: The Freshman Writing Program	3,308
Clinical Resources for Physical Therapy and Athletic Training	2,962
SLUth Search Plus (EBSCO Discovery Service)	2,638
Special Collections—Vatican Film Library	2,493
Applied Behavior Analysis	2,429
Nursing Research Guide	2,200
Social Work Policy and Practice	1,961

used in information literacy instruction for these three composition courses at SLU. This suggests that deliberate outreach to specific user populations is a driver of guide awareness and guide use. We therefore recommend that promoting particular guides to constituents be considered an integral part of the guide creation and maintenance process. High use of course guides in our LibGuides system also illustrates the way that many students think of their information needs in terms of courses as opposed to subjects (Gessner, Chandler, and Wilcox 2015).

We observed that many of our course guides are used in high proportion to their related subject guides. For example, our IB 316: Cultural Differences in International Business course guide was viewed 318 times during fiscal year 2014–2015 while our International Business subject guide was viewed 401 times. This suggests it is best practice to create course guides targeted to specific assignments whenever possible and name, tag, and organize them by course name and number so that students who think of information in terms of their courses can find them.

Technical support guides for university-supported software (e.g., EndNote) and electronic resources provided by the SLU Libraries (e.g., SLU's EBSCO Discovery Service) also received high use. The popularity of these guides suggests a possible need for additional technical support guides of various types, including other citation management tools, university-supported software, and electronic resources.

Low-Use Guides

Reference Portal guides are collections of reference sources and websites intended to help answer general reference questions. We have a general Reference Portal guide as well as Reference Portal guides that are focused on themes such as Catholic Resources, Colleges and Universities, Quotation Sources, and Publishers and Booksellers. These collections of links are holdovers from older versions of our library's website that included links to reference websites of various kinds. The low use of these guides—defined, like all low-use guides in this section, as having fewer than 30 views during fiscal year 2014–2015—indicates they are either no longer necessary in the age of Google or may simply need to be renamed. The literature shows that students don't have an understanding of what the word *reference* means and that may deter them from looking at these guides (O'Neill and Guilfoyle 2015). It's also possible that reference lists of this type may not be the kind of content that our users go to LibGuides to find. Previous research has indicated that students use guides primarily for accessing library databases in order to find articles (Ouellette 2011; Staley 2007).

Old course guides were prevalent among our low-use guides. This indicates that we need to establish best practices for curating course guides after the semester in which they're being used has passed. For example, they will need to be unpublished or made private after the semester ends or possibly converted into a more general subject guide. Similarly, guides that were simply collections of links to medical e-book textbooks were very low use as well. This suggests that there is no need to duplicate content that's already available via our library catalog.

When evaluating low-use guides, and making decisions about whether we should unpublish them, make them private, or market them aggressively to specific groups of patrons, there are several things to consider. First, we should consider whether these guides consist of content that is a duplication of, or similar to, content on a more popular guide that meets the same need. Second, we need to consider the publication dates of these guides. Some of them may have been recently published and that would account for their low use during the time period evaluated. Finally, we should consider views of these guides in conjunction with our search term tracking. It's possible that there is content in these guides that users are searching for, but the language describing the content, guide titles, and tags do not match the natural language terms searched by users. This is easily corrected with additional metadata.

Session Tracking

Session statistics, accessible only to system administrators, indicate unique users who visit one or more LibGuides pages. All page views must occur within thirty minutes of each other. A new session is counted if more than thirty minutes lapses between page views. Session statistics, compared to simple page views, can give a better estimate of the number of unique individual visitors to your site over a given time period.

Like the guide and homepage view data, these statistics indicate relatively sustained system use with some expected cyclicality matching the rhythm of the academic year. For example, figure 10.2 shows that September and December saw the highest and lowest number of sessions, respectively, though, on average, our system experienced approximately 175 user sessions per day. This level of consistent use is somewhat encouraging, but for an institution of our size, it may also reveal opportunities to more

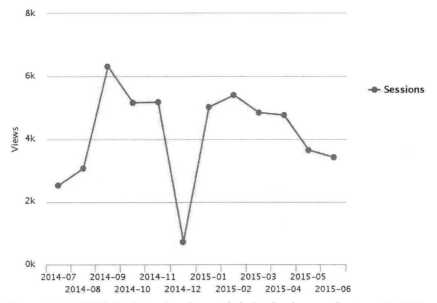

Figure 10.2.   SLU LibGuides sessions by month during fiscal year ending June 30, 2015.

effectively increase patron awareness of LibGuides and to demonstrate their usefulness since only a small fraction of our constituents are using them.

When examined in conjunction with LibGuide view data, we were able to determine that users view no more than two guides on average during a session. This further underscores the need to ensure that the guides that they do view are relevant and useful. We recommend periodically sorting the list of published guides (found on the Content menu) by the date of most recent update and identifying aging guides for review. We recommend every six months or so. For published guides, the date of most recent update may initially reflect the date of migration to LGv2 or other system-wide changes and not necessarily a deliberate change to guide content. Establishing a workflow to regularly review guides for currency will be a matter of best practice.

Browser/Operating System

Browser/Operating System (OS) data, available to system administrators, provides information about the browsers and operating systems used in combination to view LibGuides during a particular time period. Information is also provided about the number and percentage of LibGuides sessions that occurred using each Browser/OS pair (e.g., Chrome, Windows 7) as well as users' screen resolution data. We learned that while the majority of our users run a Windows operating system (64.38 percent), a significant number use a Mac (26.16 percent) and Safari as their browser (20.32 percent). This information emphasizes the need for Mac-

and Safari-related content on technical support guides, such as our EndNote and EBSCO e-books guides. We also learned that 7.85 percent of our users access our LibGuides with mobile devices. One of the enhanced features of LGv2 is that it uses responsive design, adapting as needed to fit the size of any screen. However, knowing that a significant percentage of our users access our system via mobile device emphasizes the importance of sizing videos and images in terms of percentages instead of pixels. Using relative size dimensions ensures as much content as possible is scalable and mobile-friendly.

Search Term Tracking

Search statistics, accessible only to system administrators, collect queries as entered by patrons on either the LibGuides system homepage or on various guides. Searches conducted by our users appear to fall into several general categories, relating broadly to existing content, to content that does not yet exist, and most problematically, to misunderstandings.

Existing Content

Several searches appeared to act as shortcuts for quick navigation to known guides. These searches may be by frequent users and are likely a simple way to circumvent long lists of guides in a subject category. Examples of such searches included two of our most frequently viewed guides: social work and nursing.

We also noted many searches for specific people by name, typically librarians or SLU teaching faculty. Realizing that students might tend to search by the name of their course instructor, as they do in our e-reserves system, is a good reason to include that information on course guides whenever possible. Likewise, although the guide homepage can be navigated to view guides "by Librarian," this prompts consideration of how prominently to emphasize librarian profiles on the LibGuides system homepage.

Some searches reveal opportunities for search optimization by adding additional metadata. For example, we noted several searches for "MBA," and although there is likely no need for a separate MBA program guide, we do want to ensure that those students are easily able to find the "Business Library Best Bets" guide and therefore added "MBA" as a tag. Likewise, we will sometimes consider adding common misspellings as guide tags to improve discoverability (e.g., "locovore" as a tag on the "Locavorism" guide).

Content That Does Not Yet Exist

Some searches appear to indicate patron demand for a subject or topical guide that does not yet exist. Although the system was searched nearly five thousand times in the year that we examined, the data had a long tail; relatively few search terms were repeated more than a dozen times each. Therefore, other factors will certainly contribute to the decision to create a new guide, but noticing a pattern of repeated searches should help to prioritize new guide creation. Examples that we noted referred to several popular majors like communication and theology. Others were topics or functions of broad interest like career, copyright, and LGBT.

Likewise, some searches reveal a need for new tutorials or perhaps even research methods workshops to be developed. Graduate students are likely to have strong research skills, but repeated searches for concepts like "literature review," "dissertation formatting," and "empirical articles" may mean that we have additional opportunities for outreach and services targeted to the specific needs of this user population.

Misunderstandings

It was clear from our search data that, unfortunately, many of our users do not clearly understand what they should expect to find by searching LibGuides. Some searches indicate interest in other library services and may reveal confusion between the LibGuides system and the library website. We noted examples of such searches including course reserves, ask a librarian, tour, and library evaluation by faculty (which may indicate a desire to provide feedback on collections). Information about each of these topics can be found on the main SLU Libraries website, but it is not duplicated in LibGuides.

Some searches indicate that patrons may have conflated LibGuides with our discovery system and were hoping to directly query subscription resources using the LibGuides search box. These included searches for authors, textbooks by title, and complete journal article citations. We also noted research questions (e.g., "how do parents and peers influence behavior?"), keyword combinations that reflect likely exposure to library instruction (e.g., "juvenile AND sentencing," "cognitive therapy and judith beck"), and topics which are likely too narrow to warrant their own guide (e.g., Peru SWOT, Smith-Magenis syndrome). These searches, while somewhat disheartening, point clearly to a need to describe in meaningful, patron-friendly language what LibGuides are, how they can help, and how they are different from other research tools. At minimum, we recommend installing a chat widget or other information about how to contact a librarian for research assistance on the search results page, as these patrons could benefit greatly from professional intervention. Search data can also inform library instruction, as knowledge of common misunderstandings will improve how we introduce LibGuides as a tool.

Additionally, searches that are of the "How do I . . . ?" variety could be better served by our LibAnswers frequently asked questions (FAQ) database. Again, this points to a need for descriptive language that clearly identifies what the LibGuides system contains and prominent navigation to LibAnswers from both LibGuides and the library website. Finally, there are some searches that are amusing, although not especially revealing, as it would be difficult to venture a guess about what the patron might have hoped to find. Examples include "friendship like a bucket," "spicy & winter," and "how high the fence."

It is a good idea to take note of popular searches and periodically execute them to ensure that the results are as desired. Additionally, since it is possible to view where searches are executed, librarians might be interested in searches occurring on their individual guides. For example, realizing that patrons have searched the Management guide for "glass ceiling" might be a signal that resources related to gender equity in leadership should be easily and prominently identifiable. (We are less optimistic about helping those who searched for "bayo wolf" on the Victorian Literature guide.) We intend to review search data regularly and will pass it on to interested parties in order to inform the guide creation and curation activities of our librarians.

Assets

Assets are the individual content items added to guides with the exception of rich text content. Assets include databases, links, books from the catalog, documents, widgets, polls, and RSS feeds—however, asset data is recorded for only the first four types of content listed here. Our entire LibGuides system contained more than 17,000 individual assets of various types in fiscal year 2015. These are broken down in table 10.2. Asset data can be viewed by all regular-level users and is most meaningful in the context of a particular guide. System-wide asset data is also available and may be viewed in aggregate or filtered by type. These types of data are recorded when a patron clicks through to a specific content item and can therefore indicate the perceived usefulness of suggested resources. It may also reveal the need for enhanced, patron-friendly descriptions or explicit searching instructions in order to increase the click-through rate of the asset.

As shown in table 10.2, only 25 percent of our assets (4,346) received at least a single click. It is tempting to invoke the "80/20 rule"—also known as the Pareto Principle—which implies that 80 percent of use is supplied by 20 percent of the collection (Nisonger 2008). However, we suspect it is actually a signal that many of

Table 10.2.   SLU LibGuides assets by type during fiscal year ending June 30, 2015.

Asset Type	Number
Databases on A–Z list (includes some e-reference works)	413
Links (includes unmapped databases, individual journals, and web links; does not include links embedded in rich text)	10,620
Books from the catalog (includes e-books)	6,192
Documents/files	61
Widgets	278
RSS feeds	124

our guides are unnecessarily cluttered. It is not surprising that many of the most-used resources are being clicked on in the Social Work guide—it's the most-viewed guide in our system. Our assets generated only 30,838 total clicks during the fiscal year or, on average, about 85 per day. This figure seems modest for an institution of our size; it suggests that LibGuides are not particularly efficient at directing patrons to our subscription databases.

Databases and Links

Databases account for a large proportion of our asset use, although, due to our imperfect A–Z database list mapping, some of these resources are miscategorized as links. Links also include specific journals via Serials Solutions and web links. Together, databases and links account for 10,978 of the assets existing in our system. Approximately 30 percent (3,164) of those were used at least once and accounted for 65 percent of all click-throughs to resources. This suggests that many subject guides could be designed to simply emphasize the most clearly relevant databases and perhaps provide tutorials or search tips for them, rather than attempting to provide an exhaustive list of possibly useful resources. The data also indicates that while patrons can and do use LibGuides to access subscription resources, they are less likely to use them to discover freely available web links.

Despite frequent solicitations from external website administrators, asking for their sites to be added to particular LibGuides, our data suggests that our guides are not actually very influential in directing traffic to freely available websites. In many cases it is appropriate to include website links—Census Bureau, Pew Research Center, and similar sites were frequently accessed by our patrons—but we believe that these should be very selectively curated. Extraneous links are likely to become visual clutter and, despite the good intentions with which they are presented, may detract substantially from overall guide usability. This is especially true for novice searchers (Sonsteby and Dejonghe 2013).

Books

Of the 6,176 books from the catalog in our LibGuides system, only 1,166 had at least a click or two over the period examined; the majority (5,010) had none. Of course, clicks can only be recorded for a book if a URL is present, either to its catalog record or to e-book content. It should be a matter of best practice to include URLs for catalog records when adding books from the catalog. We found that our LibGuides did not uniformly include this, but there is no asset data reflecting patron interest in these books without it.

Documents/Files

Documents/files are the least popular items in our system. Only 17 of the 61 available were used at least once during the period we examined. However, it is interesting to note that the single most frequently accessed document was the "Bloomberg Supply Chain Function data fact sheet," a vendor-supplied user guide for a specific function in one of our most technically sophisticated subscription resources. It is possible that user guides and "cheat sheets" for other specific databases might also be useful if added to relevant guides.

Data Limitations and Asset Reuse

Another limitation of the available asset data is that clicks are not recorded for embedded widgets. For example, several of our guides include embedded widgets that permit patrons to directly search our EBSCO Discovery Service. However, these searches do not generate statistics in LibGuides. Similarly, our guides include several embedded video tutorials. Although total views can be tracked in YouTube, it is not currently possible to determine when and on which guides these videos are being accessed. Also, assets that have had zero clicks recorded are not displayed in the statistics view—though Springshare plans to make such statistics available in a future release (personal correspondence, September 24, 2015). Once such statistics are available, they will be useful to identify which assets aren't being used at all. As such, librarians might want to consider removing them to avoid presenting patrons with unnecessary distractions or information overload.

Another quirk we noticed is that when searching for a specific asset, location will be identified as "none" if that asset has not been clicked on a guide. This is potentially confusing, as assets will exist, possibly in multiple locations, but appear otherwise in this view. For an accurate picture of the location of a particular asset, it is better to examine the mappings available on the content menu. This is available to all librarians. The assets view on the content menu can also be used to identify the total number of existing assets by type, which is how we were able to calculate the ratio of books and other resource types that were used.

The emphasis on asset reuse in LGv2 is most apparent in the asset statistics, as statistics aren't aggregated for databases and other assets unless they are mapped together. For example, if a specific link is added to multiple guides, it will exist as duplicate assets and have separately reported asset data for each one. This is cumbersome to interpret. However, if that link is instead reused on successive guides, the asset data will be more complete and readily usable. This is one reason that it is worth taking the time to clean up mapping of existing assets so that they are tied together. It is reasonable, to this end, to insist that all librarians add databases from the master A–Z database list when creating new LibGuides. Finally, it is important to remember that no statistics are recorded for links embedded in rich text format.

One possible use for asset data is to inform collection management decisions. A high number of clicks on a new trial database, for example, may provide an argument for purchasing it, though vendor use statistics, when available, will give the most complete information. As mentioned earlier, asset data should also be used to make decisions about carefully curating guide content. Identifying the most and least frequently used assets on a particular guide can help to streamline and declutter it. Although it may be tempting to supply patrons with a wide selection of resource options, well-curated offerings with the most relevant resources can provide a better user experience (Sonsteby and Dejonghe 2013). Likewise, identifying pages that provide the most traffic to individual assets may reveal insights about how patrons are likely using these resources.

Content Summary

A LibGuides content summary report, available only to system administrators, provides a numerical representation of the content within the site the moment that the report is run. It provides information about the number of guides, pages, content boxes, accounts, system homepage and guide views for the current year, e-reserve items, and available e-reserve storage space in the LibGuides system. It also includes the number of rich text boxes, links, files, RSS feeds, embedded media, polls, books, LibAnswers boxes, Google web searches, Google Book searches, system links, and user profile boxes in the system. It's important to note that these figures can be artificially inflated if assets and content boxes are often copied instead of being reused.

We noted that our number of librarian profile boxes seemed high (1,816). Many of our librarians include their LibGuides profile box on every page of each of their guides. The profile box would appear on the page by default when any new page was created in LibGuides version 1. This is no longer the case with LGv2, and this practice may no longer be necessary as long as the profile box of the guide owner is displayed on the guide homepage and on any pages that include information about how to get help. This change opens up valuable guide real estate for nonduplicated content. We also noted that while we have thirty-nine librarian accounts in our system, five were not being used and need to be deleted to remove visual clutter from our system-wide librarian profiles page.

E-Reserves

Additional statistics are available for institutions that subscribe to the optional e-reserves module. It provides the number of views for courses as well as individual content items within those courses. Since librarians generally facilitate access to course readings, rather than curate the content of course reserves, these statistics might be informative for course instructors. However, if low statistics are noted for a particular course or the overall e-reserve system, it may point to an opportunity for educating patrons about the system and how to use it to locate their assigned course readings.

RECOMMENDATIONS FOR BEST PRACTICES

Although many elements of site design and guide curation will vary based on institution, discipline, and intended audience, we have identified several best practices for you to consider:

- Schedule major LibGuides site revisions during demonstrated low-use months. This will be least disruptive to users.
- Use a widget or link to display only the most relevant LibGuides on specialized library websites (e.g., campus libraries or special collections). This may increase traffic to these guides.
- Promote guides to specific user populations via classroom or distance instruction. Other outreach methods may also be used to drive guide awareness and increase use.
- Design guide content for specific courses and assignments instead of subjects.
- Include the course number and instructor's name on course guides. Also provide a site-wide "browse by course" option.
- Deactivate—unpublish or make private—course guides at the end of each semester. This way only guides for courses currently being taught are publicly available.
- Deactivate low-use guides only after considering their publication dates and content duplication in other guides and evaluating system searches to ascertain whether there is content in the guides for which users have been searching.
- Deactivate guides that have not been updated in the last year and reactivate after they've been updated.
- Size media content in terms of percentages, instead of pixels, in order to make content scalable and mobile-friendly.
- Emphasize librarian profiles on the LibGuides homepage as many users search for content by librarian name.
- Prioritize new guide creation by the popularity of user searches for particular topics found in search term tracking.
- Employ user-friendly language to describe what LibGuides are, why they are helpful, and how they are different from other research tools on the library's website. Do this within the LibGuides system itself and during instruction and outreach efforts.
- Install a chat widget, or information about how to contact a librarian, for research assistance on the LibGuides search results page.
- Provide prominent navigation to LibAnswers from both LibGuides and library websites.
- Periodically note popular searches and execute them to ensure that the results are satisfactory.
- Identify and include only the most important and relevant resources on guides. Emphasize most-used subscription databases.
- Limit links to books and free websites on guides.
- Include a link to OPAC records for books from the catalog so that asset use is recorded.
- Clean up existing asset maps and in the future always add databases from the master A–Z database list. Reuse system books and links, too. This allows for easy asset use tracking.

- Delete librarian accounts that are not being used in order to remove visual clutter from the system-wide librarian profiles page.
- Review LibGuides statistical data on a regular basis—at least once or twice per year—and share findings and recommendations with colleagues.

FUTURE PLANS

Training and Support for Local Best Practices

Although any LibGuide user can view guide and asset statistics, it is unlikely that most users will realize the depth of the data without instruction and encouragement from local LibGuides administrators. After initial review of our own data, we present our summary findings to colleagues—focusing on the best practices and priority action items related to curation at the guide level. Outcomes, for example, could include identifying low-use guides that can be weeded and opportunities we've noted for new guide creation. We expect to continuously review the data and make similar recommendations at least annually.

We also plan to offer a workshop, during an upcoming intersession break, that will demonstrate the process for accessing statistics. We'll also give participants time to practice retrieving and interpreting page views as well as asset use data on their own guides. Emphasis will be on the advantages of asset reuse. It may also be necessary to give librarians assistance in mapping existing assets together, perhaps by identifying those assets with many duplicates and distributing assignments identifying their respective locations and clarifying the "original" asset ID. Although retroactively cleaning up duplicate assets will be time-consuming, we believe that it will vastly improve the overall usability of asset data in the future.

We expect varying levels of interest in statistical analysis on the part of individual librarians. However, we believe that providing support in the form of a dedicated block of time and hands-on assistance will lead to improvements in usability for our patrons. We will also consider recruiting and carefully training student workers to assist with retroactively mapping assets. Another future workshop will focus on best practices in guide design on a more theoretical level and education about the current library scholarship on guide usability.

LGv2 makes it possible to enforce a workflow that includes an approval step before publishing a new guide. We have not implemented this option; we prioritize librarian autonomy above strict guide consistency. However, we do plan to develop several new course and subject guide templates as a way of supporting our colleagues and encouraging compliance with local best practices.

Further Data Analysis

During the course of this data analysis project, we realized that we had questions that were not directly addressed by statistics natively available within LGv2.

For example, our attempts at search optimization would be informed by knowing which guide a patron actually viewed after searching the system—did that MBA student find the Business Library Best Bets guide?—or if they viewed no guide at all. This information is not directly revealed by LibGuides metrics. Because Google Analytics more closely tracks a user's trajectory and interaction with the site, we opted to implement it and will evaluate that data in conjunction with LibGuides statistics in the future.

CONCLUSION

Although the built-in LGv2 statistics do have some limitations, when considered carefully, they provide many useful insights into patron behavior and preferences. Closely evaluating our LibGuides data helped us identify opportunities for outreach and promotion to specific user groups and prioritize possibilities for new guide creation, and we learned a great deal about how our guides are actually being used and how we might improve guide usability. We also had rich philosophical discussions about the purpose of our LibGuides and the inherent tension between librarian ethos—presenting patrons with an unbiased variety of resources—versus patron preference for a simple, streamlined search experience. Data analysis alone cannot reconcile these disparate inclinations. It can, however, inform local best practices and encourage discussion about the nature of LibGuides and how best to develop and present them to our users.

REFERENCES

Gessner, G. C., A. Chandler, and W. S. Wilcox. 2015. "Are You Reaching Your Audience? The Intersection Between Libguide Authors and Libguide Users." *Reference Services Review* 43(3): 491–508.

Nisonger, Thomas E. 2008. "The '80/20 Rule' and Core Journals." *Serials Librarian* 55(1–2): 62–84.

O'Neill, Kimberly L., and Brooke A. Guilfoyle. 2015. "Sign, Sign, Everywhere a Sign: What Does 'Reference' Mean to Academic Library Users?" *Journal of Academic Librarianship* 41(4): 386–93.

Ouellette, Dana. 2011. "Subject Guides in Academic Libraries: A User-Centred Study of Uses and Perceptions." *Canadian Journal of Information and Library Science* 35(4): 436–51.

Saint Louis University. 2015. "Saint Louis University Fact Book, 2014–2015." www.slu.edu/Documents/provost/oir/Fact%20Book%202014%20-%2015%20Updated%203-Dec-2015.pdf

Sonsteby, Alec, and Jennifer Dejonghe. 2013. "Usability Testing, User-Centered Design, and LibGuides Subject Guides: A Case Study." *Journal of Web Librarianship* 7(1): 83–94.

Staley, Shannon M. 2007. "Academic Subject Guides: A Case Study of Use at San Jose State University." *College & Research Libraries* 68(2): 119–39.

V

INFORMATION LITERACY

11

Reimagining Reference and Instruction with LibCalendar

Amanda Peach, Berea College

The Hutchins Library website at Berea College underwent drastic changes two years ago. It moved from a largely hand-coded HTML site, hosted on our college server, to a new one built entirely in the LibGuides version 2 (LGv2) content management system (CMS) and hosted by Springshare. We hoped that the move would result in increased autonomy for us—granting us both more control over our content and a simplified process for managing it. Both dreams were realized due to this change. Further, we were impressed by how seamlessly we were able to integrate all of our previous LibApps content into our new website. One of the most successful of these integrations has been using LibCal to reinvent our Library Instruction Program through increased use of one-on-one reference consultations and the implementation of first-year information literacy workshops.

THE WEBSITE REDESIGN

Our library website administrator left the college for new employment two years ago, and she took all of her talent and knowledge with her. The stagnation that followed her departure was a wake-up call for those of us left behind. We found ourselves in possession of a college-hosted website that needed upkeep and maintenance— but most of us lacked the design and programming skills she possessed, as well as the server access and relationships with our Information Technology Department that she had cultivated. Further complicating things was our desire to expand and promote various instruction and outreach services via our website. We were faced with a dilemma: how could we add new content if we couldn't even properly manage our existing content?

We realized that we were out of our league after some false starts trying to update and build in the HTML site. So we chose to migrate to LGv2 CMS largely based on our existing comfort with using LibGuides version 1 (LGv1) to create course and subject guides. Every librarian employed by Hutchins had at least some experience with building in LibGuides. Our decision was also influenced by the possibilities we saw in some of the sample custom-built sites showcased in Springshare trainings and on the Springshare blog (blog.springshare.com/). We decided we would build a new website in LGv2 that included a heavily customized homepage. The training offered by Springshare, and their responsive support team, made the choice easy.

We exponentially increased our efficiency in keeping our site updated after moving to LGv2 CMS. Instead of relying on just one website administrator, as we had in the past, the responsibility was shared among three individuals: the library director, the special collections technology coordinator, and myself, a reference and instruction librarian. Our rationale was that important and timely website changes should no longer be beholden to any one individual's availability. Now site maintenance doesn't grind to a halt if one of us is on vacation or out sick. We are trusted and empowered to make needed changes in the absence of others.

The library director also implemented a weekly meeting between her and myself. This meeting is dedicated to webpage maintenance and has further improved our responsiveness. She put a placeholder for these one-hour working sessions on our calendars so that at least once a week we are forced to review the site and implement any needed changes. These meetings are called working sessions because they are meant for taking action without deliberation. Change takes place immediately whether that day's meeting is for replacing an embedded link or renaming a group of guides. These decisions are made without the approval of others—though we routinely solicit feedback from our colleagues in the library, whether formally at a library liaison meeting or library staff meeting or informally by dropping by their offices and chatting. Changes are not needed every week, but the weekly meetings combined with the distribution of responsibility have ensured that pressing website issues never languish for more than a week without being addressed.

Instruction librarians were involved in discussions regarding the content and purpose of the new site from the beginning of our library homepage redesign project. Hutchins Library is a teaching library, and library instruction is well-supported by the library administration. The middle of the library's homepage—prime real estate—was promised to Reference and Instruction to promote their services. A help box was added immediately beneath the search box, as seen in figure 11.1, which linked to our many LibApps. This includes: "Ask the Library," the public face of LibAnswers; "Text the Library," the LibAnswers SMS service; "Email Us," also routed through LibAnswers; social media links to our Facebook and blog; links to our LibGuides by subject; and "Schedule an Appointment," the link to LibCal's My Scheduler. We also added a constantly updated "Hours Box" that displays our daily hours, by department, to the left of the help box.

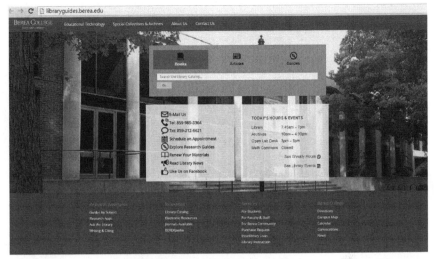

Figure 11.1. Hutchins Library's redesigned homepage.

CHANGING INSTRUCTION PRIORITIES

The One-Shot

The library's instruction team was revamping the instruction program at the same time that the website was being redesigned. We felt frustrated by the limitations of the one-shot instruction sessions that constituted the bulk of our instruction efforts. One-shots are named as such because they often represent our one and only chance to reach a group of students in a given semester. These sessions are typically fifty minutes in length but hours long in ambition. We attempt to acquaint our students with resources unique to our library, as well as provide them grounding in research techniques and theory, within that small time frame.

These sessions represent a loss of class time for the regular teaching faculty who have allowed us to enter their classroom and so we cannot typically impose on them to ask for additional class periods. One session is all we've got, so it is our one shot to teach them everything we think they should know. We frequently found ourselves discouraged by the impossible task of making sure that just one fifty-minute session was actually useful and relevant to every student in attendance—each of whom brought with them different research topics and different levels of research experience.

A few of our teaching faculty, sharing our concern, had been requiring one-on-one reference consultations for students in their classes as a supplement to the one-shot. One professor had gone so far as to make each of his students meet with us twice throughout the research process, thus allowing us a lot of face time with students as well as inflating our numbers of consults for the year. While the students who made use of this service spoke highly of its usefulness in completing their assignments, they were only a small group of students overall. Their feedback led us to wonder if we could successfully promote the service to the wider student body.

We decided to pilot a program in which the one-on-one reference consultation would be championed as our signature instruction service. Our goal for the pilot year 2014–2015 was 100 consultations. We met and then exceeded that goal; we had 230 reference consultations. As reflected in figure 11.2, we saw some drop-off in the number of instruction sessions faculty requested as a result of our pushing the one-on-ones. Some faculty opted out of instruction entirely and instead asked their students to seek us out on their own time.

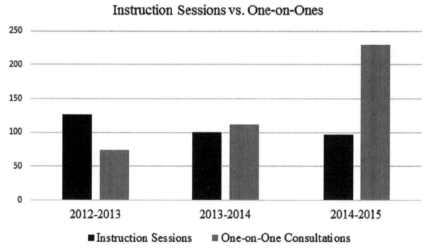

Figure 11.2.   Instruction sessions vs. one-on-ones.

Student Reference Consultants

We added student reference consultants to the mix as part of this pilot. Believing in the power of peer-to-peer learning, our library director had a vision of training talented and experienced reference student assistants to provide one-on-one reference consultations to their classmates. Berea College is a labor college. This means every student who attends receives 100 percent free tuition in exchange for working ten to fifteen hours a week. We employ student workers everywhere on campus—from the President's Office to our organic farm.

We strive to give students deep and meaningful work experience that complements their liberal arts education and makes them uniquely suited for life after college. That is no less true in the library. It is the expectation that talented students in any labor department on campus should have opportunities for increasingly more skilled and responsible levels of work. So as a part of the pilot, we developed a student labor position that would allow our proven workers to secure a pay raise and teaching experience by becoming reference consultants. We felt confident that some students would prefer to seek help from their peers rather than a librarian, and so we saw the addition of student reference consultants as a way we might reach students who were otherwise reluctant to use the service.

Student reference consultants are required to work at the reference desk for at least one year prior to taking on clients of their own. Further, they have to have completed extensive training during that first year of employment. Mentoring and job shadowing are a large component of that training. They are never left alone at the reference desk during the first semester in their position. They are instead paired with a more experienced student worker, who serves as a mentor, or with a reference librarian whom they can shadow on the job. New student workers are given time to simply observe, absorb, and ask questions about the work being done by the experienced students or librarians.

Self-paced online tutorials also play a large role in their training. These address everything from reference best practices (e.g., how to conduct a reference interview) to overviews of specific resources (e.g., the freely available training tutorials from database vendors such as EBSCO). The tutorials combine videos, written text, and quizzes. Hands-on training exercises are the final component of the new student worker training. These are done during labor meetings and during spontaneous meetings with the reference labor supervisor. Exercises include items such as practicing database searches, utilizing the microfiche collection, and generating appropriate search terms. These exercises begin with a prompt derived from a previous real-life reference question or from an assignment provided by one of the teaching faculty.

Student reference consultants had to be invited into the consultancy program by their supervisor. Not every student has the personality for teaching or the aptitude for high-level research, and so ultimately the supervisor had to determine who best fit these roles. The students who serve as one-on-one reference consultants are the best of the best. This program was a success: 12 percent of our consultations were provided by a student reference consultant in our first year of implementation.

Defining the One-on-One

Our reference desk is staffed by either a librarian, a highly trained student assistant, or both during every hour that the library is open—approximately ninety-two hours per week. It is a dedicated reference desk and therefore separate from circulation, tech support, or any of the other services that are sometimes folded into reference at other institutions. It may seem strange that we saw a need for a dedicated consultation service when students can just drop by the reference desk anytime we are open and receive immediate help. It made sense for us because we see the walk-up reference question as distinct and different from the consultation.

Devin Savage, assistant dean of assessment and scholarly communication at Paul V. Galvin Library, differentiated between the reference consultation and a trip to the

reference desk in a paper he shared at an Association of College and Research Libraries (ACRL) conference in 2015. He noted that the reference consultation is made
by appointment and requires some planning and forethought on behalf of the user.
The advanced notice also allows the librarian or student consultant to prepare for the
meeting as opposed to being caught unaware. At Hutchins Library, we have found
that this lead time allows staff members to consult with their library peers, which is
especially useful when assisting a student with their senior capstone in an unfamiliar
discipline. Appointments also allow enough time for students to be really heard and
guided to their best learning outcomes.

Our experience has prompted us to build on Savage's definition. The one-on-one
is most easily defined by how it is different from a typical reference transaction. As
students queue up at the reference desk, often in a hurry, interactions can begin to
feel more like bank teller transactions. They grow efficient and impersonal out of
necessity. Students often feel rushed by those waiting behind them and opt for quick
answers instead of complete ones. Conversely, the one-on-one is a conversation with
time allowed for give and take between the consultant and the student. It is easy to
see patrons as customers who have come to acquire answers at the reference desk.
However, in the one-on-one, the patron acts as a peer and partner in discovery. The
consultant gauges the student's prior knowledge and then starts there, inviting the
student to apply research strategies to their specific research question. Brainstorm-
ing is done together; the consultant and the student can debate over the quality or
relevancy of potential sources and ask each other questions along the way. Unlike
exchanges at the reference desk, which other employees or patrons might interrupt
with questions of their own, reference consultations are held away from the public
service point so that students receive undivided attention.

Information Literacy Workshops

As we considered how to reach more students via the one-on-ones, we also con-
templated how to reach more first-year, first-semester students overall. We knew,
based on the results of the Higher Education Data Sharing Consortium (HEDS) Research Practices Survey, that a large percentage of students arriving at Berea College
had a deficit in one or more basic information literacy skills. The HEDS Research
Practices Survey, currently used at more than eighty colleges and universities, asks
students about their precollege research experiences and assesses their information
literacy skills (www.hedsconsortium.org/research-practices-survey/). The survey
measures students' knowledge of—and comfort with—skills such as finding sources,
evaluating sources, using information, and citing sources. Our institution has ad-
ministered this survey to the incoming class each summer, prior to their arrival, for
several years. We use the results to, among other things, inform the curriculum of
our first-year library instruction program.

Previously, most sections of the first-semester general studies composition class,
GSTR 110, shared a similar assignment: the documented essay. Further, the second

course in the general studies sequence, GSTR 210, required all sections to write a ten-page research paper. Both of these assignments required a certain level of proficiency with the skills measured by the HEDS survey. It was easy for us to make a case for library instruction, as a component of the first-year general studies curriculum, based on the deficits revealed by the HEDS survey. We therefore enjoyed nearly 100 percent buy-in from the teaching faculty for several years regarding library instruction. We used the time allotted in our one-shot instruction sessions to introduce these new students to the basic concepts identified in the HEDS survey.

The focus of the GSTR 110 course began to change over the past year or so. It moved away from the documented essay and toward a focus on reading for comprehension and other writing forms such as free writing and timed-response writing. There was not always room for our one-shot in this new iteration. We built our instruction program to support a curriculum that was no longer being taught anymore, so it made sense that faculty didn't want to give us a class period if we were no longer relevant to their assignments. Nonetheless, the information literacy skills deficit persisted. We knew there was still a need to be met—but where?

It would have been possible to hold back on all library instruction until the second semester since there was still nearly 100 percent buy-in for library instruction there—because of the common research paper. However, we felt strongly that we would be doing our students a disservice to wait that long. What if they had a research-focused course their first semester, such as any of the introductory social sciences courses, and found themselves ill-equipped for the research process?

Our solution was to do a second pilot project one year later, running concurrently with the continuing one-on-one project, in which we would offer workshops on three separate information literacy topics. We adapted eighteen questions from the HEDS survey and then grouped those questions into three larger categories: finding sources in the library, evaluating sources, and knowing when to cite. We graded the responses of every incoming student and then let their first-semester general studies professors, who are also their advisors during their first year, know how they performed.

We made recommendations for each student based on their results. They either needed to take one, two, all, or none of our workshops. We asked advisors to pass this to each student and to also encourage them to participate in the workshops because the skills they would hone in these workshops would allow them to be more successful during their time at Berea. This was done with the support of the dean of curriculum and student learning.

We chose to limit the workshops to thirty minutes. This included the time needed for an exit assessment. We needed less time because the workshops covered only one-third of the material that was covered in fifty-minute one-shots. Further, we thought they should be short enough that committing to attend would not be too large a burden on the students who were, for the most part, attending during their free time. The focused nature of the sessions made them less frantic in nature. This left enough time to move from the stale but efficient demonstration/worksheet model to time-consuming but less predictable active learning techniques.

According to the *Greenwood Dictionary of Education*, active learning requires students to "regularly assess their own degree of understanding at handling concepts" and is characterized by "attainment of knowledge by participating or contributing" (Collins and O'Brien 2011, 6). Examples of active learning techniques include activities such as using discussion and debate, polling students (whether electronically with clicker software or informally with raised hands), and collaboration for problem solving. Our instruction team committed to the idea of implementing engaging active learning techniques—in part due to the influence of professional literature in our field, but also because of knowledge gained via professional development training at the Association of College and Research Libraries' Immersion Program Teacher Track (www.ala.org/acrl/immersion/teachertrack). Two of our librarians are alumni of that program.

Knowing we would have only a half hour per workshop, but that our activities could quickly grow unwieldy with too many attendees, we decided to focus on smaller workshops. We capped the workshops at fifteen students each. This was made easy by LibCal because it allows you to set a limit on the number of registrants for any class or workshop and, once it is full, it is closed to other attendees. We made the registration form accessible from a LibCal public calendar called "GSTR 110 Workshops," linked in our "Hours Box" on the homepage.

MY SCHEDULER AND THE ONE-ON-ONE

Though we had prior experience with providing one-on-ones, we had always found them to be a logistical nightmare. It might take five e-mails back and forth with a single student just to nail down a time when we could meet. It was not a sustainable model if we truly wanted to increase usage. When considering how to expand the service, the lack of a systematic approach to scheduling them was our biggest obstacle. Fortunately, the My Scheduler feature removed the need for meeting time negotiations. Instead, students could search for the availability of a particular librarian or for an ideal time slot that met their own availability and schedule themselves.

The reference librarians each committed to a certain number of hours that we would be available per week. The full-time instruction librarians agreed to offer a minimum of five hours per week: ten thirty-minute time slots. Our student reference consultants were asked to offer two hours (four consultation slots) per week. We include slots during the night and weekend shifts. As hard as it is for a librarian working forty hours a week to match their schedule to that of a student in need of assistance, it is exponentially more difficult for a student worker who only works ten to fifteen hours to match theirs to that of another student. Fortunately, once we provided our student research consultants with My Scheduler accounts, they were able to block out office hours of their own, making the one-on-one attainable for them.

SCHEDULING ONE-ON-ONES

Initially, when students chose to follow the "Schedule an Appointment" link, they were taken to a LibGuide in which each instruction librarian's individual profile appeared. These profiles included an embedded widget that linked to that librarian's personal calendar. This arrangement was problematic. The side-navigation layout, to which we had committed in LGv2, required users to scroll down four or five page lengths just to see all of the profiles listed. Users never did that—they stopped at the first librarian or maybe the second and ignored the others listed below. This meant that the bulk of the work was laid upon just the first librarian.

After a semester of imbalanced workloads, the link for "Schedule an Appointment" was changed to redirect to My Scheduler's public page, which shows everyone's availability simultaneously, as shown in figure 11.3 below. The instruction team immediately noticed a difference in the way in which the appointments were scheduled, and work became more evenly distributed across the available librarians and student consultants.

Figure 11.3. My Scheduler public page for scheduling an appointment for a reference consultation.

Another trend that we noticed was the popularity of our night slots. Evening slots, offered from 6 p.m. until 9 p.m., were consistently the most booked. These were followed by Sunday hours (2 p.m. until 9 p.m.), lunchtime hours (11:30 a.m. until 1 p.m.), Friday afternoons (2 p.m. until 5 p.m.), and finally by any other hours during the business day. These findings may be unique to our campus, but they have remained consistent over our four semesters offering the scheduled one-on-ones. Our status as a residential college may affect these time preferences. Nearly every student lives on campus, so it is not an imposition for them to remain on campus after classes. Further, the library is just short walk—three to eight minutes—from anywhere on campus and is convenient for our students to access.

The fact that we are a labor college may also contribute to students' time preferences. Since each student must work a minimum of ten hours per week and many labor positions operate during normal business hours, many students struggle to squeeze their work hours in between classes. Nighttime, lunchtime, and weekend consultation hours are a necessity for them.

WHY LIBCAL?

There are other online scheduling systems you could consider, so why should you choose LibCal? For us, an obvious benefit was that it would seamlessly plug into our existing LGv2 website. It is important to us that our students not feel like they are getting the runaround. As we redesigned our website, we tried to limit the number of links students would have to click in order to accomplish a task. We did not want to send students to resources outside of the library to accomplish tasks unless we absolutely needed to do so. The research process—and the library—can be intimidating enough as it is.

LibCal looks like, and speaks to, the other apps we are using. Students don't ever have to know that they are negotiating different products. When we tried to hand-code a few of our LibApps products into our previous HTML site, the results were embarrassingly unprofessional-looking. Using LibApps in LibGuides, however, results in a polished and attractive appearance. Further, we have one less login to remember since LibApps uses a single login for every app in the suite.

There are a number of other benefits, perhaps not unique to LibCal, that make the service indispensable to us. We rely on the push notifications to keep us organized. Each time a student makes an appointment for a reference consultation, an e-mail is sent to their consultant, and then the consultant pushes that notification to their Outlook calendar. This ensures that they don't forget their commitment. It also means that the schedule peers see, when trying to schedule other library meetings and events, reflects their true availability.

LibCal also stores all of your events online. This means even if you delete a notification by accident, or if Outlook is down and you cannot access it, you still have a copy of your schedule online. LibCal allows users to customize the scheduling form in My Scheduler; the reference consultant can ask students for insight into their information need prior to their arrival and then prepare accordingly. The registration form for workshops offered via the public event calendar is even more customizable. Both the event calendar and My Scheduler allow you to elect to send out automatic reminders to students prior to the consultation or workshop. Whether it is because of the reminders or because they have taken ownership of their learning by scheduling the consultations themselves, we have found that we have far fewer cancellations and no-shows using My Scheduler then we ever did prior.

PROMOTING THE SERVICES

We have used a variety of tactics to promote the one-on-one consultation service. The most important is linking to the service from the center of the library's homepage. We have taken advantage of that location's visibility to introduce the service in every single library instruction session. Further, we promote it to our teaching faculty, in the hopes that they will pass it on to students in need. We attended faculty in-service training, prior to the beginning of the academic year, and used that opportunity to make faculty aware of the service at both a poster session and at departmental meetings. We advertise on our library Facebook to make students aware of the service and to shine a spotlight on the profiles of individual student reference consultants. Word of mouth and return visits by students we have worked with previously are still some of our biggest sources for appointments.

Information literacy workshop promotion consisted of presenting faculty with an overview at the fall faculty conference. Additionally, each first-semester advisor was given a list of their students and their performances across the three competencies. Specific workshops, as appropriate, were suggested for each student. Faculty were also asked to suggest attendance to their students. Reminder e-mails promoting the service, generated by both the library director and the dean of curriculum and student learning, were sent to the first-year advisors periodically throughout the eight weeks that the workshops were offered.

RESULTS

Student feedback regarding reference consultations has been incredibly positive. We sent out brief surveys to our consultation customers asking about their experience during the spring of 2015. Fifty-five students responded. When asked, "How useful was the One-on-One Reference Consultation appointment in completing your assignment?" 70 percent found it "Very Useful" and 30 percent found it "Useful." When asked, "If you scheduled your reference consultation via LibCal, how easy did you find it to use?" 81 percent found it "Very Easy" to use. Students praised the service when asked for additional comments or feedback—providing accolades such as "I wish I would have utilized reference consultants throughout my college experience" and "This was one of the most helpful things that I have done in my time at Berea. Thank you."

We measured the information literacy workshops' impact by comparing participants post-test quiz results to initial pre-matriculation scores. Our goal was to have 80 percent of all students pass each of the quizzes—either initially or because of workshop intervention. We fell short of that goal, from between 14 percent and 22 percent depending on the competency measured, but we did see significant improvement across all three competencies. Table 11.1 reflects the change in incoming students' pass rates—comparing initial survey results and post-test results. Students who attended the workshops had passing rates between 82 percent and 100 percent. Our workshops definitely had a positive influence on students' ability to demonstrate competency across all three information literacy areas as measured by achieving at least a 70 percent on the exit assessment.

Table 11.1. **Student performance on information literacy skills test by component.**

	Finding Sources	Evaluating Sources	Knowing When to Cite
Percentage of students passing during summer before school started	27%	29%	51%
Total percentage of students who passed by the end of the semester	58%	60%	66%

LESSONS LEARNED

We experienced some growing pains in our first few semesters as we were unprepared for how popular the consultation service would be. Nonetheless, it taught us valuable lessons. We learned that individually, consultants should only offer as many potential meeting time slots as they can actually handle. It sounds simplistic, but sometimes we offered more slots than normal because it was near midterms and we wanted to be more flexible in order to accommodate our students during their time of greatest need. We expected that some of our typically empty slots would remain so and that some of the new offerings would be filled instead. As luck would have it, though, for at least one of our consultants, there were multiple weeks when nearly every single slot would be booked. This included newly added ones. That time commitment, combined with scheduled classroom instruction, reference desk shifts, and liaison responsibilities, became overwhelming. The lesson learned was to schedule yourself in such a way that you would survive if every single slot was booked. You never know—it just might happen. Additionally, appointments need space built in between them. The one-on-one is a discussion, and discussions never wrap up tidily in perfect thirty-minute increments. This can be accomplished by purposefully choosing available slots that are at least two consultations lengths apart or by updating the "appointment padding" area of the My Scheduler "Appointment Scheduler Settings" with extra time.

We also learned that using scheduling software means you have one more thing you need to remember to update when you are out of the office. Two of us went to a conference, remembering to update our Outlook calendars and arranging to have our reference desk shifts covered while we were traveling out of town, but forgot to update our availability in My Scheduler. Students scheduled appointments with us while we were out because we didn't delete those time slots. This left us in the embarrassing position of having to cancel and reschedule.

We learned equally valuable lessons through our experiences with the information literacy workshops pilot project. The majority of students attended because their professors required it. We hoped that students might choose to take advantage of this opportunity to learn—required or not—because our experience with the one-on-ones had shown us that students were willing to participate in programs not directly tied to extrinsic rewards. Unfortunately, the workshops did not enjoy the same popularity as the one-on-ones. Several professors requested one-shot sessions centered on the workshop curriculum and had all of their students attend whether they needed to or not. The most heavily attended workshops were those offered in the evenings—followed by those offered on Sundays and near lunchtime. Due to this, we will probably reduce the number of morning workshops we offer in the future.

We saw students procrastinate in scheduling themselves to attend. They had eight weeks of workshop offerings to choose from, and most of them waited until the last three or four weeks to schedule. We had double the number of workshops available during the first four weeks, believing naively that students would schedule early just so that they could get them over with. Next time, we will probably do the opposite, offering either at least as many—or perhaps more—in the second half of the eight weeks as we did in the first. We are also considering ways of promoting directly to the students rather than relying on their advisors to encourage them. Our goal next semester is to hand out personalized cards to each student that informs them which, if any, of the workshops we would like them to attend. We have also considered e-mailing students directly and promoting the service via social media more heavily.

Finally, and most importantly, we saw a direct correlation between the number of students in attendance and the performance on the exit assessment. Pass rates for two of the three skills components fell as the number of participants in the workshop increased. For example, only 82 percent of students who attended a larger one-shot class dedicated to finding sources passed. Ninety percent of those attending a smaller finding sources workshop passed. Table 11.2 reveals a similar difference for the evaluating sources workshop.

Table 11.2. Students who passed information literacy skills survey by format.

	Finding Sources	Evaluating Sources	Knowing When to Cite
Percentage of students who attended workshop and passed	90%	85%	100%
Percentage of students who attended class and passed	82%	78%	100%

We speculate that location played a role in this. The small workshops were taught in the same space as reference consults, with all of the participants and the librarian gathered around a medium table that could seat no more than six. There was no place for students to hide in such a setting. They were forced to participate by the physical intimacy of the situation. The small size also meant there was time for anyone who wanted to talk or ask questions to do so. In the large classroom setting, used for group sizes bigger than five, it was much easier for distracted students to go unnoticed or undetected. Also, students attending the workshops they had scheduled themselves may have been more intrinsically motivated than those who were forced to attend as a part of a class. Going forward, we would like to cap the workshop size at an even smaller number than fifteen and avoid entire classes attending a workshop-themed one-shot instruction session. Five students per workshop would be ideal.

CONCLUSION

Migrating our website to LGv2 CMS allowed us to create a website that reflects our priorities as a teaching library and emphasizes tools for student learning. Our new website incorporates the LibApps that we have come to depend on to organize and streamline our work processes while adding sophistication to our website functionality. LibCal has made the largest impact; it has allowed us to reimagine our instruction program and add new ways to meet and teach our students. LibCal has empowered us to efficiently and systematically offer new instruction services that we know have the power to positively impact student learning.

REFERENCES

Collins III, J. W., and N. P. O'Brien (Eds.). 2011. "Active Learning." In *The Greenwood Dictionary of Education*, 2nd ed., 6. Santa Barbara, CA: Greenwood.

Savage, Devin. "Not Counting What Counts: The Perplexing Inattention to Research Consultations in Library Assessment Activities." Paper presented at the annual meeting of the Association for College and Research Librarians, Portland, OR, March 2015. www.ala.org/acrl/sites/ala.org.acrl/files/content/conferences/confsandpreconfs/2015/Savage.pdf.

12

Using LibGuides to Create Modular Library Research Lessons for Distance Learners

Melissa Cornwell, Norwich University

We decided to transfer the Norwich University Kreitzberg Library for Online Students, a customized website for our online student population in the College of Graduate and Continuing Studies (CGCS), to LibGuides in the summer of 2014. Our online student population is composed of both degree completion and graduate programs. These students are all working adults or serving in the military, so courses are built with an asynchronous learning model and do not meet face to face or at a certain time online. Library instruction also has to be built with an asynchronous learning model while providing the same direction and structure as instruction done in a face-to-face or hybrid learning environment.

Our shift to LibGuides included redesigning all of our instructional materials. Among these were our Library Research Lessons (LRLs)—in-depth research tutorials that are used in three of the online graduate programs. These were created and implemented in two courses across three graduate programs. This chapter looks at how the Kreitzberg Library used LibGuides version 2 (LGv2) to re-create the LRL instructional component with a focus on sustainability and accessibility.

THE KREITZBERG LIBRARY FOR ONLINE STUDENTS WEBSITE

The Kreitzberg Library for Online Students is a website built solely for the online student population at Norwich University and is separate from the website used by our on-campus students. Since there are different services for the on-campus students that are not available for the online students, the decision was made to keep separate websites so as not to confuse the two different populations. For example, online students are not able to request interlibrary loan items from other libraries and there is a greater emphasis on using online resources. The online students get more tailored support with guides that feature resources and instructional content specific to their program.

This website was originally built with Drupal and had a webpage for each of the different programs. Drupal is a free, open-source content management system used to make websites. The Drupal site also worked with the Angel learning management system (LMS) used by CGCS. The library hosted the Drupal site on its own server, and regular maintenance was completed by the head of Digital Services. The library felt it was time to move the online student website to a new platform when CGCS announced that it would be moving to the Moodle LMS. Additionally, the Drupal site had become hard to manage, and we already used LibGuides for on-campus guides via LibGuides CMS.

The project started in LibGuides version 1 (LGv1) but then moved to the beta site for LGv2 in June 2014. Four LGv2 features made it easier for the library to maintain the new online students' website in LibGuides: groups, the new centralized asset management, the new shared library in the image manager, and the new side navigation option. We used different group settings for the guides that constituted the online student website, as well as to create unique templates used solely for the Kreitzberg Library for Online Students guides. The librarians were also able to ensure that all website branding would be consistent with that of the CGCS by using new templates.

LibGuides was the perfect choice for hosting the new website for two important reasons: responsiveness and accessibility. LibGuides uses a "responsive mobile-friendly design" that is also ADA compliant (Springshare, Inc. 2015a). Responsive design would allow students to view the guides on their smartphones and tablets. ADA compliance would also make it easier for students with disabilities to view and interact with the content.

A Kreitzberg Library content box was added to the Moodle classrooms. It featured a drop-down menu with links to each of the different program guides. Students could also just click the "Visit the Library" link. Links were placed directly in the classroom, and boxes were added to the program guides for those that featured instructional content.

We created guide development best practices and collected them in a LibGuide to improve all of our guides and to maintain consistency in appearance and structure. The best practices guide featured standards for guide creation as well as box and content standards (guides.norwich.edu/best/box-content). It also addressed other items of importance such as adding images, video, and storage guides. Examples of these best practices include:

- Per the Web Style Guide, optimize your images before uploading them. Optimization entails compressing and resizing your images to reduce their size and increase page speeds; large images can slow down the browser's ability to download a webpage. By optimizing photos, librarians can also ensure that the quality of the images is maintained and is not distorted or pixelated:

- ○ For PNGs (what most screenshot software creates): tinypng.com/.
- ○ For JPEGs, PNGs, and GIFs: kraken.io/web-interface.

- Upload from your computer or reuse an image already stored in Image Manager. Please remember to add an ALT tag for screen readers in the provided field—ALT tags are added at the guide level, not the image level. ALT tags are important for complying with ADA regulations as they explain an image even if a user cannot see it. The Image Manager is a feature in LibGuides that allows librarians to upload and collect images that they will then use in their guides.
- Do not set a pixel-defined width or height on your image. This will make it distorted if the box is not large enough or if the user is on a smaller screen. Either keep the image at its full size and plan for it to fill the box or edit before uploading.
- You can see and organize all of your uploaded images anytime under *Content>Image Manager*, as well as from LibApps.

These standards helped keep the images consistent across all guides and to ensure that they worked on mobile devices. We did something similar for adding videos:

- To add a new video:
  - ○ Copy the YouTube URL into Embed Responsively: embedresponsively.com/. This tool allows a librarian to make a responsive embed code for a video or other media item, which means the video will fit within a webpage and will be viewable no matter the size of the page.
  - ○ From a box in your guide, click Add/Reorder and select Media/Widget.
  - ○ Give the video a distinct name so that others will be able to easily tell what it is (this will not display on the public side).
  - ○ Copy and paste the amended code from Embed Responsively into the embed code field. Add an s to http (https) in the website URL part of the code. This will allow you to see the video within the LibGuide as you edit it, which you can't usually do because of the security certificate used by LibGuides.
  - ○ Save it and test your responsive video embed!

- To reuse an existing video:
  - ○ From a box, click Add/Reorder and select Media/Widget. All of your videos exist as Widgets.
  - ○ Select Reuse Existing Widget and search for it.
  - ○ Save! Remember the title of the widget will not display, so you may need to add Rich Text above it or name the box it is in accordingly.
  - ○ Note you can browse existing widgets in *Content>Assets* by limiting the Type column to Widget.

- A note on Closed Captioning
  - ○ If a video has Closed Captioning (CC) on YouTube, the necessary parameter is not automatically added to the embed code.

- ○ Within the <iframe></iframe> tags add the following: cc_load_policy=1. To find the iframe tags, you would have to go to the embed code for a video (which you can find in your Assets). All videos exist as Widgets so you would be altering the code in the Widget. When you click to edit the Asset, you should see the place for the Embed Code; this is where a librarian can alter the iframe tags.
- ○ The above will add the CC button to the embedded video play bar and have it set to ON. The viewer can turn it OFF.

The other best practice that we used was creation of storage guides. These were internal guides shared among the librarians that featured pages or boxes that could be mapped to other guides from one central location. This made maintaining the content easy as the librarian only had to change the content in one guide and it would push out to the other guides through the mapping feature. This best practice was particularly useful for building the LRLs and other instructional guides.

- Many commonly used boxes are available in the Storage Guide. Please reuse these boxes to ensure ease of maintenance when changes are necessary. Please keep the boxes linked; do not copy them. . . . Some of these items are also available as Widget Assets so they can be included in boxes along with other items—these specifications are on the Storage Guide.

BACKGROUND ON LIBRARY RESEARCH LESSONS

The LRLs are in-depth research tutorials that are used in three online graduate programs: history, military history, and diplomacy. Previously, these lessons were long video tutorials due to the limitations of our Drupal site. We updated and expanded these lessons when we moved to LGv2. We also tied the LRLs to class assignments and discussions—as well as requiring them as part of student coursework—to increase their relevance.

The LRLs are placed in the beginning weeks of the seminar to prepare the students for their assignments that are due in the later weeks. For example, the Intro to Diplomacy Research LRL is completed in week two to help the students prepare for their week five essay. The distance learning librarian made the LRLs relevant to students by using assignment topics to demonstrate example searches in our databases. This librarian also e-mails the students in each course section, a week before the LRL is due, to remind them to complete the tutorial.

The LRLs for the history and military history programs are required in the MH510 Introduction to History and Historiography seminar. This is the first eleven-week seminar that students from both programs take together. During this seminar, students are required to complete the Intro to History Research LRL in week three and the Finding Primary Source Materials LRL in week five. These research lessons help the students to complete their preliminary bibliography, which is due in week three, as well as their annotated bibliography and final research paper, which are due in the final weeks of the seminar.

The LRL for the diplomacy program, Intro to Diplomacy Research, is used a little differently. The diplomacy program offers two different first seminars that students are able to take. Subsequently, this means that the LRL could not be implemented in the first seminar. Instead, the Intro to Diplomacy Research LRL is used in the third seminar for the program, GD530 Economics and the International System, which all diplomacy students are required to complete as part of their core curriculum. As previously mentioned, students are required to complete the LRL in week two of the seminar. It is tied to an assignment, due that same week, and helps them prepare for their week five essay.

Requiring the LRLs to be completed as part of student coursework has proven beneficial for them as they progress through the program. Further, students frequently return to the LRLs even after completing it in their first course. Four new LRLs are currently being planned for three other master's programs: public administration, information security and assurance, and nursing. The LRLs for public administration and information security will both be placed in the first course students take in their respective programs. LibGuides has contributed greatly to the success of our LRLs due to its many options for design and development.

DESIGN AND DEVELOPMENT

When first designing the LRLs, it became immediately clear that sustainability and easy maintenance were key factors that needed to be considered. The online seminars run continuously; there is a very small window of two weeks in which a librarian can review the LRLs and update them if necessary. Easy maintenance meant using the same videos and content across multiple LRLs for different programs, but the LRLs also needed to be program-specific for context and relevancy. We decided to include more general research concepts videos toward the beginning of the LRL and more program-specific information toward the end.

The first decision to be made was on the layout and structure of content. Since the student population is composed entirely of adults, content structure needed to promote self-directed learning to match the asynchronous learning style taking place in the CGCS classrooms. LGV2 came with an option for not just the top tab navigation on a guide but also the new option for side navigation. The librarians found that the top tab navigation wouldn't work for the design and flow we needed. Side tab navigation, however, allowed for a more linear scaffolding structure for the content.

Content was broken into small modules with short videos and text or screenshots. Students could go from one module to the next, and each would build upon the last. Each module, or page, would also focus on only one research concept (Smith 2010). The distance learning librarian decided to go with a one-column side navigation template only, instead of two columns, for the LRLs. This simplified the guides and kept them from looking too cluttered.

The scaffold structure for the modules was imperative, but we also needed flexibility. The goal of the smaller research modules was to have the students advance through them at their own pace without the risk of being overwhelmed by the information (Martin and Martin 2015). The modules were meant to build on one another—however, the content was structured so that students could pick and choose which modules they wanted to complete. If a student was proficient in one step of the research process, he or she did not necessarily need to complete that module.

The new side navigation template features also provided multiple ways for the students to move through content. Previous and next buttons, a new feature in LGv2, were added to each module to create a sequential—but flexible—flow. We also added box-level navigation, another new feature in LGv2, to provide more ways to navigate each research module.

We included either video or screenshots in each module. Videos specifically are used to explain general research concepts and are created using Screencast-O-Matic or Captivate. We uploaded these to YouTube in order to add closed captioning and meet ADA compliance. The distance learning librarian tried to keep the videos shorter than three minutes (Bowles-Terry, Hensley, and Hinchliffe 2010), though the longest had a four minute and forty-two second run time.

The items we create have to be responsive, like our LibGuides site, per our standards for creating boxes and content. We needed to take steps so that nonresponsive items would meet this standard. Videos had to be altered when added to our assets in order to address this. The distance learning librarian copied the YouTube URL of our videos into the Embed Responsively tool (embedresponsively.com/). Students could now access the LRL on a mobile device and view videos within the appropriate guide. A text transcript of the video was placed under each video to further comply with ADA standards. Thus, each video module consisted of a responsive video and a text transcript.

A series of research videos, about general research concepts and building a research strategy, had already been created for on-campus students. These addressed topics such as:

- What are Databases?
- Developing and Analyzing Your Topic
- Choosing Keywords
- Constructing Your Search
- Refining and Broadening

Centralized asset management in LibGuides made it easy to reuse these videos since they were already being used in on-campus guides. These five general research videos were added as the first items for the Intro to History Research and Intro to Diplomacy Research LRLs. Other videos that were created for each Intro LRL included a meet-your-librarian video, a video on defining a research strategy, and a video on how to mine bibliographies for sources.

Another LRL, Finding Primary Source Materials, was different in nature from the other two LRLs but still had the same navigational structure. The librarians also worked with University Archives and Special Collections to include videos on finding primary sources in archives. Additional topics addressed here include:

- What is a Primary Source?
- What is a Secondary Source?
- What is a Scholarly Source?
- What is a Popular Source?
- Before You Start Searching for Primary Sources

Screenshots, and not videos, were used to show the students how to search databases. Since databases change their interfaces a little every year, it was easier to update screenshots instead of videos with every interface change. The librarians developed a sample research topic that was broken down into keywords in order to create context and relevancy. These were then used to search the most relevant databases for the respective programs. For example, the Intro to History Research LRL uses the same topic and keywords to search JSTOR, America: History and Life Full Text, Historical Abstracts, and the Military and Government Collection.

All screenshots and/or images had to be placed in the Image Manager before loading them into the guides per our established content standards for images. Librarians had to delete the set pixel-defined width and height of each image, which could only be done as they were added to a guide, in order to make the images responsive. The distance learning librarian also decided that each step in searching a database should have its own box and that there would only be one screenshot per step. For example, in the Intro to History Research LRL, separate boxes and screenshots were created to show how to conduct a search and how to review the search results. The last page on each LRL has links to other helpful guides and contact information for the reference librarians at the Kreitzberg Library.

ASSESSMENT

Assessment of student learning has been difficult due to the nature of the content in the LRLs. The majority of the videos are shared across multiple LRLs, which makes it harder for the librarians to assess which students from the different programs are watching which videos. We can collect guide views, using the Statistics feature in LibGuides, and review the total for an LRL guide as well as views for each tab/page of the LRL. We also collect video views from YouTube. These two methods are the only way for us to see how many students view the content from the history and diplomacy programs. The Statistics feature in LibGuides also makes it easy for us to collect views on each of the guides used in the entire online student website by separating the statistics by group. It is easy to pull up the statistics for those specific guides since the Kreitzberg Library for Online Students was already in its own group.

The distance learning librarian decided to look at other assessment methods since LibGuides views and YouTube views weren't providing much information about instruction effectiveness. In March 2015, a pilot was conducted by putting a survey at the end of the Intro to History Research LRL. The survey was created in LibSurveys, which allows a librarian to create surveys and forms that can then be embedded into a guide. LibGuides has an option to add LibSurveys Items in the list of content items. This is why we used LibSurveys and not any other survey creation software.

The survey featured a scenario-based series of questions related to the research concepts covered in the LRL. The research question that history and military history students had to address was: "What was the role of the International Brigade in the Spanish Civil War between 1936 and 1939?" This question addressed research concepts and was the same topic used to search the databases in our screenshot examples. The librarians wanted the students to respond to a scenario with a problem instead of only self-reporting on what they learned in the lesson. The distance learning librarian also wanted the students to apply the research concepts they learned in the LRL. This scenario is similar to what the students would be doing with their own future research.

The survey was built with both radio fields and text fields. A label field was included before every question so that the overall research question appeared with every quiz question. Two questions required students to fill out a text field, and three were multiple-choice questions. Springshare then added options for a welcome screen and a thank you screen at the end of the survey (Springshare, Inc. 2015b). This survey was easily embedded into the Intro to History Research LRL. Students were not required to complete it—we plan to keep optional.

CONCLUSION

The LRLs continue to be used in the coursework for our online students, and other programs have started to request them. Future LRLs are currently being planned for three other graduate programs. We also have surveys to build and implement for new and existing programs. Additionally, our distance learning librarian wants to create more complex research methodology modules to be included in the capstone studies of multiple graduate programs.

Standards and best practices for accessibility and sustainability continue to be the foci of how we design and develop instructional materials for our online students. The current LRLs have created a foundation that can be built upon in other courses—we will continue to work on and improve them in order to help develop students' information literacy skills in a manner that benefits them in future seminars.

REFERENCES

Bowles-Terry, Melissa, Merinda Kaye Hensley, and Lisa Janicke Hinchliffe. 2010. "Best Pratices for Online Video Tutorials in Academic Libraries: A Study of Student Preferences and Understanding." *Communications in Information Literacy* 4(1): 17–28.

Martin, Nichole A., and Ross Martin. 2015. "Would You Watch It? Creating Effective and Engaging Video Tutorials." *Journal of Library and Information Services for Distance Learning* 9(1–2): 40–56.

Smith, Susan Sharpless. 2010. *Web-Based Instruction: A Guide for Libraries.* 3rd ed. Chicago: American Library Association.

Springshare, Inc. 2015a. "LibGuides Features." springshare.com/libguides/features.html.

———. 2015b. "LibSurveys Update Now Live." blog.springshare.com/2015/08/13/libsurveys -update-now-live/.

VI

LIBRARY ADMINISTRATION

13

Using LibGuides to Facilitate Systematic Staff Training

Stephanie Lee Weiss, University of North Florida
Lauren Newton, University of North Florida

The Thomas G. Carpenter Library (henceforth the library or TGC) serves all disciplines at the University of North Florida (UNF). We've adopted several Springshare products both to help us in our daily work and to better serve students and faculty. Streamlined access to all of our sites, via the LibApps portal, offers our library staff an easy, convenient way to keep track of desk statistics and find answers to common questions. However, with more than fifty librarians, paraprofessionals, and student workers, how can our department leaders effectively train everyone regarding best practices and workflows for public service desk staffers? LibApps, a flipped classroom, and active learning principles; that's how! This chapter discusses our use of Springshare products for staff training and how it helped us break down barriers and work better together.

LIBAPPS AT TGC

We began using Springshare products in 2010 when the company introduced LibGuides and LibAnswers. This was done, in part, to serve more students and faculty after hours. It also provided a way to connect to our growing number of online students and any others who we may not have been reaching. Additionally, LibAnswers was appealing to us for statistics-tracking capabilities using RefAnalytics. In 2011, LibChat was released, and we added that product to our lineup. We also got a second, private LibGuides site, which we'll call "Intranet" in this chapter. Later, we adopted LibCal for study room reservation as well as one-on-one research consultation scheduling.

THE NEED FOR A SYSTEMATIC APPROACH TO TRAINING

We were appointed by UNF Library administration to lead the respective product implementation teams for LibAnswers and LibGuides. Part of our charge was to introduce the systems and train staff to use them. We had some success with a combination of lecture/demonstration and hands-on activity. However, after a couple of years, and the introduction of our internal LibGuides site—our Intranet—four things became clear.

First, due to the nature of student positions on college and university campuses, someone was training student workers basically all the time. Secondly, some staffers either had never fully bought into the benefits of using LibAnswers and LibGuides or had forgotten their initial training. This was particularly evident through transaction review, or lack of transaction entry, in LibAnswers and LibChat. Thirdly, knowing how to use our Intranet was going to be required for all regular library faculty and staff going forward. And lastly, LibGuides and LibAnswers upgrades were on the horizon. This would certainly necessitate more widespread training than had occurred in the past.

We also experienced a number of retirements and new additions to the staff at that time. One of those new hires was a director of public services. The director met with all of the staff and librarians during her first few months at the TGC. She asked, among other things, what they would like to see in the near future and how she could help them achieve their professional goals. One request was echoed by many—training—not just on Springshare products but also for a variety of systems and topics relevant to academic library work in public services.

INITIAL TRAINING

Changing information landscapes and technology affect job roles for public services staff. Many of our services have adjusted to accommodate this shift but not all of our staff have done so—either because of technological wariness, resistance to change, or some other factor. Our initial LibAnswers and LibGuides adoption was a major culture shock for some librarians and paraprofessional staff. As mentioned, many staffers had requested training on certain aspects of library work that they wished to learn or felt they didn't know well enough to provide good service. It was clear that something had to be done so that we could all be more consistently good at, and feel comfortable with, our evolving jobs in the modern academic library.

The public services director appointed a team to develop and deliver training sessions based on input from staffers and those topics the director deemed top priority. The team, which consists of two veteran instructor-librarians (the authors) and the head of access services, also recruited other subject matter experts (SMEs) to either deliver training or to work with us to develop a session based on their own in-depth knowledge or established best practices.

We began in 2013 with a "summer intensive"—a series of topics delivered once per week, over seven weeks, during the summer when it has traditionally been less busy and would be a bit easier to gather large numbers of staff away from service desks. Most of the seven topics were designated high-priority for an effective library service desk such as standards for customer service or keeping statistics. Nearly all of these topics had been addressed with training previously.

However, there was evidence that some staffers were still not getting the message. Others were willfully ignoring directives to improve interactions with patrons or to use tools such as LibAnswers and RefAnalytics. The director wanted to incorporate an assessment component to address this. There had also been some shifting of positions, changes in job duties, and new hires, so the director decided that whether they were veteran librarians, new paraprofessionals, student workers, or somewhere in between, everyone in public services would be required to attend the training sessions.

Sessions during the summer intensive consisted mostly of lecture/demonstration with a little practice thrown in for good measure. Assessments were generally completed at the end of each session. We employed a variety of assessment types to try and inject some novelty into the training. For example, we borrowed our Center for Instruction Research and Technology's set of classroom clickers to do real-time, low-stakes quizzing. Clickers are small hand-held devices that look like a simple calculator. The few buttons correspond to letters and numbers that allow the user to enter a selection and send it to the facilitator's computer for collection and sometimes to display the results. This exposed many library staffers to a tool they'd had no occasion to use previously, and folks enjoyed the ability to answer questions in this way. We also had a couple of librarians engage in some behavior modeling and role-playing—which was probably more entertaining than it was effective.

USING LIBGUIDES TO TRAIN AND MAINTAIN

Since we needed a place to keep track of the schedule and any documents needed for training late-night staff, we used our internal LibGuides system. We call this our Intranet. We use this to store handouts, presentation files, and links to free online webinars of interest. We also tried to create training materials that could be used at any time when new employees came to work at the library. In the fall of 2014, we began our upgrade to LibGuides version 2 (LGv2) and the first thing to change was the Intranet. We also began integrating some more complex research tools into the session topics. Only librarians had been sufficiently trained on LibGuides before then, so we took the opportunity to begin using the Intranet a little differently.

First, a guide name change: the training program was retitled Public Services Professional Development Series to reflect and convey to staffers the true nature of the program—to assist folks with—and sometimes drag them to—improvement in their professional capacity at the TGC. Second, although we had been training and refreshing folks on our various Springshare products periodically, a new directive to create process manuals in the Intranet necessitated a thorough training on LGv2 for everyone. So why not use Springshare products to train people on the Springshare products?

We used the new LGv2-based Intranet to train people on how to use and build guides. Our instant message (IM) reference service is performed with LibChat so we used LibChat to train folks on IM reference services. The learning activities consisted of staffers creating boxes, with certain kinds of information for the LGv2 Intranet sessions, and sending and answering IM chat questions for the LibChat sessions. These are systems that everyone, regardless of position, is expected to know and use. And it means that the systems function as both the training tool and the tool to be trained. Folks become familiar with how patrons interact with the tools while learning how they will interact with them as library employees.

Taking a page from the instructional design best practices playbook, we looked for ways to make training more engaging while ensuring that it would stick with staffers long afterward. There were also still some issues with folks retaining and using the information, concepts, and desired actions modeled in previous training sessions. To curb this, the director and the training team decided to remove assessment from the training session and get people using the tools workshop-style. The assessment now takes place a week or more after initial training to give time for staffers to internalize and practice tasks in real-life situations.

We also wanted to try out the flipped classroom concept, in order to devote more time to active learning rather than covering basics that could be read or watched ahead of time. As defined by Educause, a flipped classroom is "a pedagogical model in which the typical lecture and homework elements of a course are reversed" (2012). In the context of our flipped classroom environment, participants are required to view readings, videos, and subject-matter LibGuides prior to class. We then devote the live session to practicing the material.

Using a flipped classroom style for staff training has several advantages. For example, prior knowledge is respected. If the staff member already has content mastery prior to the workshop, they will not need to sit through an introductory lecture. As an added bonus, those staffers who are proficient with the content are especially helpful to have in the workshop session because they can impart wisdom and experience to colleagues for whom it still may be new material (Attebury 2015; Nichols Hess 2014).

Flipped classrooms save precious staff time by allowing folks to view the videos or readings whenever they have a chance to fit them into their busy schedules. This is easier than requiring a large group to be together for a lecture when everyone has meetings and desk shifts to attend. Plus, staff are given time to contemplate and process the material prior to the workshop. It encourages them to think of examples of when they had a patron question on this exact topic or perhaps some tricky situation for which they would like the facilitator's input. This makes the workshop more personal and meaningful. Staffers are motivated to learn the content prior to the workshop because they know it will help them to perform their jobs more effectively (Attebury 2015).

We developed learning outcomes—the end goals for what a staffer should be able to do after training—and a rubric for each topic. We used these to craft both the exercises participants would do during the sessions as well as the assessment activities. See figure 13.1 for an example of learning outcomes and a rubric. Rubrics are posted in a Rubrics box on the Public Services Professional Development Series guide. The guide is organized into pages, or tabs, based on semester as well as a few additional tabs for outside webinars of interest.

CampusGuides

Objective:		Excellent	Intermediate	Needs Work	Comments
As a result of this training, you will leave with a guide that you can use as a practice area or you can continue to edit to meet a goal.	Locate & log into CampusGuides	• Navigates to site by at least one method • Successfully logs in	• Completes only one of the two tasks	• Unable to locate site or log in	
Outcomes: 1. Locate and log into CampusGuides	Access & Edit the Profile Box	• Accesses the Profile Box • Makes changes and updates such as uploading a photo	• Able to access the Profile box but unsure of how to make changes	• Unable to access or edit the Profile Box	

2. Access and edit the profile box
3. Create a new guide
  • Select a Group & a Subject
  • Add a page and title it
	Create a New Guide	• Demonstrates the mechanism for creating a guide
		• Assigns appropriate Group & Subject
			• Creates a guide but unsure of how to assign group, subject, or both	• Unable to create a guide or assign group and subject	

4. Add content to a guide
  • Add a box
  • Upload a document
  • Use the text editor to add content to a box
  • Add a link
	Adds Content to a Guide	• Creates & labels a new page
		• Adds a box
		• Uploads a file
		• Creates content using the text editor
		• Adds a functioning link
			• Completes one to four of these tasks but unsure of how to do the remaining task(s)	• Unable to do any of these tasks	

Figure 13.1. Example of learning outcomes and rubric for workshop using the Intranet.

LIBGUIDES AS LMS

LibGuides is a content management system at heart, but the team determined that it was actually using our Intranet site as a learning management system (LMS)—"a software application that automates the administration, tracking, and reporting of training events" (Ellis 2009). Viewed through an academic lens, our Public Services Professional Development program is a single massive "course" with a great deal of content that covers all aspects of working at public service desks.

Content chunking is recommended for course development. This is especially true in online instruction. Chunking, as the name suggests, involves breaking content into manageable pieces. It can help participants feel less overwhelmed by allowing their short-term and working memory to process and remember information more effectively (Marican 2014). Instructional designers and faculty at educational institutions might employ this strategy by creating modules, or some other unit, within a classic LMS. Indeed, there are university libraries that have used their school's LMS to successfully facilitate library staff training (See and Teetor 2014). However, librarians may not have access to the institution's LMS if they do not teach credit-bearing courses. Further, public and special libraries may not have any sort of LMS at all.

LGv2 makes it easy to modularize your training topics. Web-development skills are not necessary to create and maintain professional online content in this system. The ability to quickly and easily add multiple types of content—text, links, embedded media, document files—and organize it means that LibGuides can function similarly to an LMS. The multi-content boxes in LGv2 allow us to keep all materials for a given training topic in one place. It also shares similarities with the current course template UNF's instructional designers offer faculty for use in Blackboard.

As versatile as the system is, there are some limitations to using LibGuides as an LMS. It does not provide a traditional in-line gradebook or other confidential means for tracking assessments. This was not a hindrance in our situation because we created a workaround. LibGuides offers the ability to password-protect tab pages, whole guides, and single documents. Our team created a password-protected tab on the Public Services Professional Development Series guide that is hidden from the rest of the library staff. We used a cloud-based spreadsheet, shared only among the team members, to keep track of who had completed assessments and their performance. We used the cloud version of Excel via Microsoft Office 365, but Google Sheets would also work well.

LibGuides itself does not offer a way to give online assessments, but there are practical solutions. LibSurveys offers the ability to craft forms and surveys that can be integrated into your guides (Richards 2015). We use this tool for a variety of purposes, though it can be used to create short quiz-like surveys or to provide staffers an option to give feedback on training sessions. The information generated from the forms and surveys is only accessible to their creators, their designees, and system administrators.

CONCLUSION

We knew that the authority of management, in this case, the director of public services, was key to participation. As Aizenshtat et al. observed with their own staff training program, the director's presence in the sessions, as well as her provision of snacks, set the tone for the training (2015). Our professional development series is required for everyone who works on a public service desk, and each workshop covers a different topic that is essential to providing high-quality service. No one is exempt. This approach addresses inequalities among the staff, be they perceived or real (Straatmann 2008). Additionally, by requiring all staff to attend, we've begun to implement an organizational mentoring culture to prepare for changing roles and possible promotions (Munde 2000).

The public services staffers, particularly those whose primary duties are not research-based, have become their own learning community within our larger group (Nichols Hess 2014). One unexpected but pleasant surprise has been the peer mentoring that takes place. Folks who don't really work together, other than the fact that they are in the same department, are helping each other learn new skills and tools. For example, when staffers were given the task of creating a handbook or process manual in the Intranet for their daily job functions, one quiet paraprofessional picked up the system quickly and became the go-to for colleagues who were struggling to get the hang of content types within the boxes in LGv2. Another interesting development is that people seem happier about attending training sessions. Collegiality and collaboration have begun to form a cycle. And there have recently been requests to attend the Public Services Professional Development sessions from faculty in other library departments.

Making the switch from a lecture/demonstration model of one-off sessions to a flipped classroom with active and collaborative learning facilitated by LGv2 was invaluable. By engaging in activities that promote analysis, synthesis, and evaluation, participants are dynamically involved in their own learning. Real-world simulations and role-play of actual questions or research topics presented by patrons—and using the Springshare products to answer them—allowed staffers to learn both the Springshare systems as well as the library best service practices set forth by the department.

Don't have an instruction background? If you work for an academic institution, visit your instructional designers or e-learning specialists. Whether you plan to conduct your training in person or online, they will have plenty of good advice for designing your sessions for maximum impact and ensure that you use proven techniques. If you don't have ready access to academic instructional designers, check with your company or municipality to see if there are any training specialists in human resources or a similar department. Or check your library's collection and the Internet for books and other resources on the topic. Taking time to learn a little could save you headaches later.

If you have LibAnswers and LibChat, we recommend mining your database for patron questions and chat transcripts for real questions fielded by staffers. We did that and also provided actual research questions from consultation requests to create scenarios for TGC staffers to practice. While they aren't expected to get all the way through a complex research question, paraprofessionals and student workers in public services at the TGC must be able to assist patrons in beginning their research. They should be able to direct patrons to relevant research tools, particularly if librarians are not available for immediate assistance. Provision of real-life examples and scenarios in training, plus the ability to collaborate with a partner and use the tools, have boosted confidence and made a difference in everyone's performance.

Using LibGuides as an LMS has made it easier to train those who work late-night and weekend shifts. Using recording/screencasting software in conjunction with this can also facilitate training across campuses or for telecommuting employees. We use Camtasia. However, depending on your needs, you could use free software online such as Jing or Screencast-O-Matic.

It's also handy to have a YouTube account for storing and linking to the videos. While it's not advisable to upload video files to LibGuides, it's very easy to embed YouTube and other videos into boxes. These are then posted with the other documents in the guide so that all materials are easily accessible anytime. This method means that new hires don't have to schedule training time with busy colleagues unless they have questions or need additional information.

LibGuides promotes reusability and shareability. This has indeed come in handy when creating our pre-workshop content. We have linked to whole guides and re-used boxes of content originally created in our public-facing LibGuides system. The ability to add this existing content into the Intranet saved us time and also showcased some of our work by encouraging staffers to look at the public guides and use them in their work with patrons. We managed public services training, but another library unit could easily copy the Public Services Professional Development Series guide for the structure, even if they didn't need the same training topics or materials. And although our guide is internal and will not be shared at this time, one could easily share a public staff-training guide with the LibGuides community.

Active and collaborative learning models help students retain content and improve critical thinking skills. So why not apply these methods and other adult learning theories in a library staff training program? Utilizing LGv2 while training people to use them has proven to be a giant step in the right direction for our staff. We are well on the way to reaching our goal to help TGC employees deliver the excellent service that today's patrons have come to expect from their modern academic library.

REFERENCES

Aizenshtat, Marla, Stacy Bruss, Catherine Wagner, and Briget Wynne. 2015. "In-House Training on New Library Processes at the NIST Research Library: A Case Study." *Reference Librarian 56*(1): 59–66.

Attebury, Ramirose Ilene. 2015. "Adult Education Concepts in Library Professional Development Activities." *New Library World 116*(5/6): 302–15.

Educause. 2012. "7 Things You Should Know About Flipped Classrooms." net.educause.edu/ir/library/pdf/eli7081.pdf.

Ellis, Ryann K. 2009. "Field Guide to Learning Management Systems." ASTD. www.td.org/~/media/Files/Publications/LMS_fieldguide_20091.

Marican, Fareeza. 2014. "Basics of Content Chunking." www.slideshare.net/fareezam/basics-of-chunking.

Munde, Gail. 2000. "Beyond Mentoring: Toward the Rejuvenation of Academic Libraries." *Journal of Academic Librarianship 26*(3): 171–75.

Nichols Hess, Amanda. 2014. "Byte-Sized Pieces: Equipping Academic Librarians to Integrate Technology into Library Instruction through Manageable, Maintainable, and Meaningful Staff Development." *Internet Reference Services Quarterly 19*(3/4): 283–96.

Richards, Talia. 2015. "Springshare Buzz: Power Your Library Website with Libguides CMS: Libsurveys." buzz.springshare.com/producthighlights/libguidescms-as-website/features/lib surveys.

See, Andrew, and Travis Stephen Teetor. 2014. "Effective E-Training: Using a Course Management System and E-Learning Tools to Train Library Employees." *Journal of Access Services 11*(2): 66–90.

Straatmann, Michael. 2008. "Addressing Perceived Inequalities between Academic Library Faculty and Paraprofessionals through Staff Development Programs." *Nebraska Library Association Quarterly 39*(1): 3.

14

Not Just for Students

Noninstructional Applications of LibGuides

Lance Day, MSW, MLIS, Samford University
Carla T. Waddell, MLIS, Samford University
Jane C. Daugherty, MLIS, Samford University
Lauren M. Young, MLIS, MA, AHIP, Samford University

Samford University (SU) began the fall 2015 semester with 484 teaching faculty, an enrollment of 5,206, and eleven degree-conferring schools and colleges (Samford University 2015). Samford students' academic careers and the academic faculty and staff's library requirements are supported by the Harwell G. Davis Library (SU Library), the Lucille Stewart Beeson Law Library, the Career Development Center, the Curriculum Materials Center, and the Samford University Center for Healthcare Innovation and Patient Outcomes Research. SU Library is operated by administrative, cataloging, circulation, collection management, acquisitions, interlibrary loan, reference and research services, special collection, and systems departments.

These divisions work together to effectively maximize a license agreement for LibApps that includes extensive use of LibGuides. This is used as both a tool for guiding students and academic staff to library resources and for creating inward- and outward-facing guides that streamline communication and data sharing with library faculty, staff, student workers, and other affiliated groups.

SU has appointed a reference and research services (RRS) librarian as the Lib-Guides administrator who facilitates making LibGuides accounts available to all interested library staff and faculty. Each user has the option to utilize the product and is encouraged to be creative yet develop within the limits of best practice. The guidelines for creating guides are informal if not creating for broad student access. However, best practice does dictate color scheme and overall appearance for public and private guides. We agreed that a design guide was needed, and its initial development was based upon providing a location to access predesigned boxes that encouraged uniformity. It has since developed into a best practice guide.

SU Libraries upgraded to LibGuides version 2 (LGv2) in January 2015. After this, a workshop was conducted to highlight new features included in the upgrade, encourage usage, and outline best practice guidelines. A wide range of guides existed prior to this and were migrated during the update. Since then, numerous guides have been created for things such as departmental homepages, conference homepages, faculty search committees, special projects, policies and procedures, how-to guides, and employee training.

A large part of successfully maximizing and integrating LibGuides at SU has been learning to informally ask the question "Does a LibGuide enhance a given project?" This is not a formal process as much as it is something that organically occurs during conversations. At times it is a useful tool, and at other times it does not seem like the best course of action to support the project being considered. Guides described as being inward-facing are intended for internal library purposes and utilized by library faculty, staff, and students. Outward-facing guides are designed to communicate information to larger external audiences that includes library patrons. Each of these categories will be described in this chapter. LibGuides used for nonacademic purposes at SU are organized into the following categories:

- individual library staff LibGuides: inward-facing,
- individual library staff LibGuides: outward-facing,
- department-level LibGuides: inward-facing,
- department-level LibGuides: outward-facing, and
- project and event-related LibGuides.

INDIVIDUAL LIBRARY STAFF LIBGUIDES

Inward-Facing

One of the ways that SU Library has maximized its LibGuides license is by utilizing the resource for individual library staff pages. The inward-facing individual library staff guides at SU can best be described as private spaces for individuals to use for professional purposes. They are not private in the sense that they are password-protected, but they are "hidden" and one must have the link in order to access them. This section discusses the opportunities for faculty and staff to organize annual review, promotion, and portfolio documents as well as collate bibliographies and create test/demo pages.

Promotion and Tenure LibGuides

A common inward-facing option at SU is utilizing a guide to organize annual review, promotion, portfolio documents, and academic writings. Promotion and tenure portfolios are an important component of most academic librarians' careers. These compilations need to be simultaneously comprehensive and concise. They must contain documents that provide an exhaustive summary of professional activities, publications, and service in the appointed time frame, along with supporting documentation and correspondence to highlight noteworthy projects, honors, and achievements. The promotion timeline generally spans a number of years; a librarian will not know which accomplishments will serve their portfolio best when it's time to submit, thus the challenge of collecting, saving, and organizing supporting documentation in a stable, intuitive environment.

LGv2 allows for the development of private pages for the purpose of organizing and storing documents in one location. Akin to other cloud storage systems, the information is not device-dependent and can serve as a primary storage location or as a backup to another system. As with guides developed for other purposes, sections can be created for specific timeframes, projects, types of documentation, images, multimedia, and anything else that might be required for a promotion or tenure portfolio.

The authors created a guide like this using a single page with a tabbed type box and then labeled the tabs Curriculum Vita, Annual Review (for each year), Promotion, and Academic Writing Projects. The CV tab contains a CV saved as both a Word document and as a PDF. Each annual review tab contains the final annual review in a Word document for the given year. In the current year's tab is a copy of a working Word document that will serve to inform the librarian's annual review—it is updated throughout the academic year. At the end of the year, this is used to compile the librarian's annual review. It is then archived after the review is completed and all feedback has been finalized. A new working document is at that point created for the upcoming year. The Promotion tab contains all documents related to the SU Librarian promotion process and a link to the SU Library Promotion Roundtable LibGuide.

Research- and Project-Related LibGuides

LibGuides can serve not only as personal repositories for completed publications but also as research tools. Librarians working on research projects can create a guide devoted to all of their projects. Useful applications for this include creating bibliographies of consulted resources and attaching PDFs for personal reference and use, attaching drafts in chronological order in order to trace edits throughout the revision process, and sharing the private link with colleagues and collaborators as a space to share and access materials. Some institutions have restrictions on file-sharing services. LibGuides institutions can safely use these licensed spaces for these purposes without running afoul of policies and prohibitions.

Test and Demo LibGuides

Another application of personal, private LibGuides is to use them as test and demo pages. Many librarians have liaison responsibilities to departments and curate guides to serve the needs of those patrons. SU Library faculty and staff utilize test/demo pages for exploring potential projects. This is a space where users can engage the product and explore resources in order to enhance their skills and ensure that best practice is being exercised. A number of unpublished guides exist at SU with names such as Play Zone, Sandbox, and Trial LibGuide. These contain images and other elements that are often used in public guides.

Opportunities abound for LibGuides to interface with other institutionally licensed resources such as learning management systems, but it can take some trial and error to create widgets that display and behave in the intended fashion. Internal guides serve this function—librarians can create widgets, share them with colleagues, and practice exporting and importing them. We recently created a personalized "AskMe" widget that liaisons can add to their departments' Moodle course pages as a means of contact. Librarians can import the template widget from the shared internal LibGuide into their "sandbox," edit it to their liking, and push it out to their department when they are happy with it. It is valuable to have the space and opportunity to edit and test before launching.

Outward-Facing

Having just detailed some private, inward-facing uses for LibGuides at SU Library, let's explore some other applications. Still internal in nature and intended for library faculty and staff access, these guides are not confidential and are authored by librarians for use by colleagues. Examples include: guides to share research, publications, and presentations with library colleagues; guides to relay information to colleagues from conferences and meetings; and guides that serve as a homepage for news and information communicated with colleagues.

Professional Development and Conference LibGuides

In the previous discussion of inward-facing individual guides, an option available to librarians utilizing them for research purposes was to share their private link with colleagues and collaborators. Similarly, finished projects are presented using outward-facing guides to share research, publications, and presentations with library colleagues. Countless hours are spent writing papers and designing posters. Often, colleagues do not have the opportunity to appreciate this work in the primary context (e.g., articles published in journals to which the library does not subscribe, posters presented at conferences that no or few fellow colleagues can attend).

Librarians are always eager to share their research efforts with the profession, and our in-house colleagues can best appreciate the subject matter. Access to conference proceedings is increasingly limited to badge-holding attendees, which further limits collegial access to research. Short of e-mailing the internal library group numerous attachments, how can librarians share their efforts?

SU librarians are creating LibGuides, accessible by colleagues, which contain this information. We have shared information presented and obtained at three different conferences. The librarians e-mailed the library faculty listserv links to these guides upon completion. These links can also be shared with the wider library community or directly with conference organizers for attendees interested in learning more about a given presentation. See figure 14.1 for an example of a conference overview LibGuide.

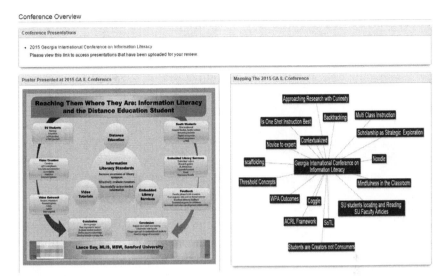

Figure 14.1. SU Library Conference Overview LibGuide.

Newsletter LibGuides

Another method used to communicate internally at SU is a monthly instruction newsletter that is housed in a LibGuide. The link is sent out to the library faculty listserv when a new issue is posted. The guide serves as an archive for previous issues should librarians wish to refer back to the statistics, quotes from surveys, and best practice tips contained in each issue.

DEPARTMENT-LEVEL LIBGUIDES

Inward-Facing

LibGuides are effective for internal departmental use as they are well suited for gathering data, sharing policies, and posting manuals and training documents. The primary purposes of existing departmental guides vary between instructional and informational. Assessment is a permanent fixture in the world of academic libraries for both collecting and sharing statistics, and LibGuides can help streamline the process.

Cataloging LibGuide

LibGuides serve the SU library cataloging department as a means of tracking daily cataloging statistics. Catalogers use an internal guide for step-by-step instructions on how to collect statistics from the LMS and OCLC, along with usage and collection statistics for general and special collections. Each system or collection has a tab. The guide creator includes screenshots as visual aids when deemed useful.

Assessment LibGuide

Another inward-facing departmental guide aids in the collection of annual statistics. Each tab is designated for an office or accrediting agency to which SU provides reports (e.g., IPEDS, ACRL, annual campus reports). This guide facilitates the collection and reporting process each year by including step-by-step directions for pulling and calculating the statistics by item as required per accrediting body. LibGuides makes it easy to combine narrative directions, detailing where the statistics are recorded, with easy-to-review tables for the calculations.

Librarian's Assessment Portal LibGuide

The Librarian's Assessment Portal is an inward-facingpage within Library Instruction and Assessment that serves as a gateway for librarians participating in instruction initiatives. It includes the necessary links to the LibAnalytics tools that allow instruction librarians to record and reflect on each class instruction session, run reports on previous instruction, and review the instruction reports from previous years. The Assessment Portal also includes a section for planning, which provides novice instruction librarians with instruction scripts, best practice guidelines, a template for instruction correspondence, and other instruction tools. Finally, there is a box on the right side of the page that links to all relevant LibAnalytics reports.

Reference Student Workers LibGuide

SU Library has created LibGuides for student assistants. It is an easy way to share the information that student assistants need in order to be successful on the job. The SU Library Reference and Research Services Department created such a guide, as depicted in figure 14.2. The Home tab is set as an introduction to the department and includes links to tools: time clock, how to use the time clock, how to check their work schedule, and contact information. Guidance is provided about when and how to refer questions to a librarian, and links are provided to both the university and library student worker handbooks. The second tab contains training resources used to train student assistants. This includes training lists, duties, daily tasks, opening and closing procedures, and information detailing when to send a question on to a librarian. The third tab, "When Can You Work?" is used for gathering scheduling information from the students.

New Employee LibGuide

SU Library uses an internal private LibGuide for all new employees as a way to share library culture FAQs by assigned mentors when meeting with their mentees. An example is provided in figure 14.3. The guide contains useful tips for the campus and local area. The "Working at Samford" box guides Samford employees by providing links for institutional resources and tools. Examples include the institutional e-mail signature template, links for emergency alerts and campus initiatives,

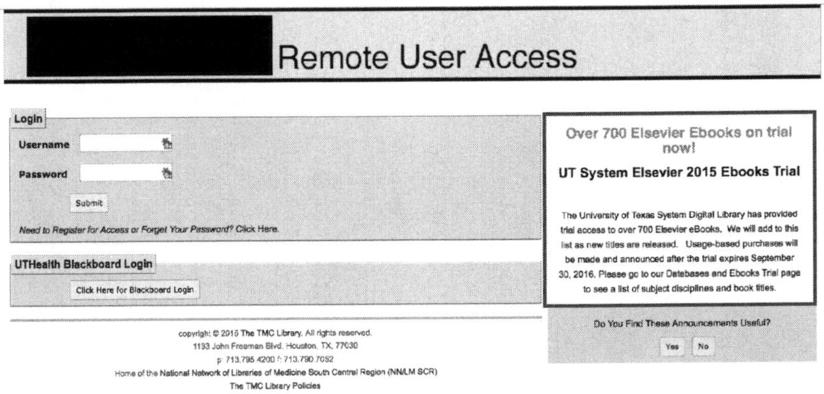

Figure 14.2. **SU Library Reference Student Assistant LibGuide.**

and links for daily campus life such as using the print shop, dining on campus, and technology assistance.

Even more important for a new employee is a box designated for Working at the University Library. Sometimes it is the little things, like understanding how the employee kitchen is cleaned, that can make a big difference. However, understanding the internal committees, mission and history, policies, organizational charts, and maps is also important.

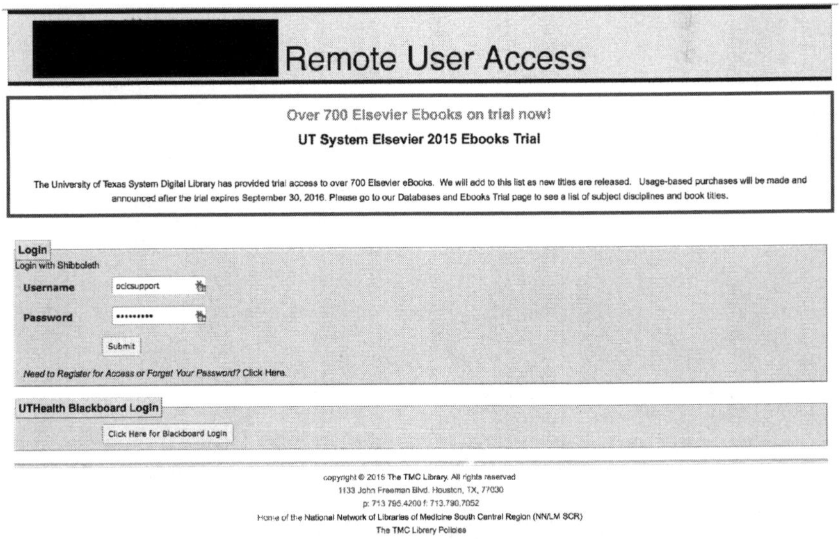

Figure 14.3. **SU Library Orientation and Training for New Employees LibGuide.**

Outward-Facing

Government Documents LibGuide

SU also uses private LibGuides for internal departmental information. Guides are not only utilized for sharing training resources; several SU library departments house policies, procedures, and referential lists along with training documents. An internal departmental guide was created for Government Documents to aid in the training of staff and student assistants and to serve as a central location for all of the referential lists. The following tabs are offered in the guide: the history and scope of our collection; Federal Depository Library Program (FDLP) and Government Publishing Office (GPO) background, historical, classification, and processing tutorials and information; a referential list of cataloging, processing, and collection development handbooks, manuals, and regulations for maintaining a depository collection; listservs; tasks and projects for interns; ongoing projects; and a preparation list for IGHR (Institute of Genealogy and Historical Research). This guide serves as an example of cross-over guides in the SU collection, which serve both internal library needs and patron needs.

Interlibrary Loan LibGuide

LibGuides can be used as a homepage for departments that require instructions and explanations, such as the Interlibrary Loan (ILL) Department. SU Library's ILL LibGuide serves as a place for university faculty, staff, and students to retrieve more information about how ILL services work and provides a way to get to know who is in charge of acquiring the items and how the ILL network functions. Selecting "Interlibrary Loan" under the "Services" section of the main university library homepage leads to this LibGuide.

The front section of the ILL guide gives a brief explanation of who can utilize ILL services and how ILL works. It also includes a direct login to the ILL system for those who wish to access the service immediately. This LibGuide includes a Profile section that features the Interlibrary Loan coordinator and her contact information. This feature provides a face for the service and personalizes the process, which is especially beneficial for internally managed departments like this one. Other linked sections on the ILL page include: ILL Policies, Your ILL Account, FAQs, Faculty/Staff Delivery Service, and Policy for Partner Institutions. The architecture of this LibGuide lends itself to easy-to-follow navigation and departmental transparency.

Library Instruction Services LibGuide

Another option listed under "Services" on the University Library webpage is "Library Instruction." This leads to the guide especially designed for university faculty to make instruction appointments with librarians via a LibAnalytics form. This includes options for preferred dates of instruction, librarian selection, and different types of instruction, among other necessities for customizing instruction according to the needs of each class. "Library Instruction" is a catchall term that includes a spectrum of informational services, from scavenger hunts meant to encourage exploration of the physical library space to research instruction specializing in using individual databases for specific courses and disciplines. This page includes links to an instructional video on how to use the form as well as general specifications for scheduling instruction. The instruction coordinator's direct contact information is provided, in addition to a rundown of the services offered and the mission of the instruction program.

The menu tabs at the top of the page link to individual pages that include: Policies, Information Literacy, Assessment Standards and Evaluation, Library Assignment Principles, Library Assignment Tools and Examples, Faculty Resources with links out to ACRL standards, Statistics (which links to LibAnalytics instruction reports), the two most recent Standardized Assessment of Information Literacy Skills (SAILS) reports, and the Librarian's Assessment Portal.

PROJECT AND EVENT-RELATED LIBGUIDES

Search Committee LibGuides

SU Library makes a basic template guide available for search committee use that is meant for members only. A box is set for the candidate evaluation tool, job description, and individualized Qualtrics surveys for library employees to rate each candidate. Other boxes are added that contain each candidate's information: cover letter, CV or resume, and their list of references.

Another temporary private guide is created once the search committee has identified candidates for campus interviews and is only available to library faculty and staff. It includes the schedule for each candidate's visit, links to the candidate's letter, CV or resume, list of references, suggested questions, and their presentation topic. Links to Qualtrics surveys are made available to library faculty and staff after candidate presentations have been held. This is deleted after the search committee has reached a decision.

Deselection LibGuide

The designer of this guide researched the deselection process prior to the project and discovered another academic library had created a deselection website. This was in response to academic departments expressing concern about books being deselected. The librarian overseeing our project was aware of the importance of transparency. Consequently, she chose to elevate scholarly communication about the deselection element of collection development and viewed it as paramount to the success of the project. It was deemed that a Deselection Project LibGuide would be the most necessary instrument to meet this goal.

The deselection guide was developed with an emphasis on being able to parse relevant information with tabs. This structure allows a creator to generate a layered structure that can be accessed based on a user's level of curiosity. This guide includes the following five tabs: Home, Criteria, Blog, Lists, and "What happens to the books." This is designed to introduce academic faculty to deselection while also inviting them to participate in the process. The Home tab is organized with one box that discusses the rationale for the deselection project, one that covers a "Did you know" section that outlines "The continued shift from print resources to electronic . . . ," a box that outlines the current status of the project, and a profile box with a photo to indicate the librarian in charge of the project.

The Criteria tab delves deeper into the process by providing detailed criteria for the current deselection project. At this point a faculty member should be able to gain more knowledge about the process and begin embedding themselves in the deselection conversation. The third tab is linked to a blog that delivers updates regarding the project. The blog also allows interested faculty to ask questions and make comments. The idea behind creating a blog was to generate an interactive location for frequently asked questions to live. As a user follows the tabs from left to right, the goal of organizing information in a logical manner becomes evident.

If a faculty member has investigated the first three tabs and arrives at the fourth tab entitled "Lists," they can choose to evaluate the actual lists of books that are being considered for deselection. These files are organized by call number in order for faculty members to directly access and evaluate books relative to their discipline. The page also contains a link to the Library of Congress Classification Outline if users need to determine where their discipline is categorized.

In the case of a collection development project that specifically seeks input from SU faculty who use the collection, it was necessary to password-protect the Excel files that contain lists of books slated for deselection. This was accomplished by using EZproxy. With EZproxy in place, a user is required to access these files with an SU-specific username and password. In addition, the Excel files can be updated throughout the deselection process and notes about these updates are easily added.

The final tab, "What happens to the books," outlines the varied options for books after deselection. This includes library book sales, Better World Books, recycling, and opportunities for books to be relocated to a specific department. If a member of the campus community is interested in relocating deselected books to a specific department, then a conversation about this process will ensue. Finally, the guide serves as an archived account of the process should questions arise after completion.

Each department at SU was notified via a campus-wide e-mail about the deselection initiative and directed to the University Library Deselection Project LibGuide. This message was also resent as a reminder for faculty to provide feedback about the books being targeted for removal. This guide received the highest number of views when these e-mails were sent, with 150 views after the first e-mail notification and 123 after the follow-up e-mail. The LibGuide has been viewed a total of 593 times at the time of writing.

IGHR LibGuide

The Institute of Genealogy and Historical Research (IGHR) was launched in 1962 with five faculty members and roughly forty attendees. IGHR and the university have evolved over the years. The Institute now involves more than thirty faculty members and more than two hundred students. IGHR was first advertised and organized via newsletter. As it grew, the necessity for a website arose. Then as the website became too large for the library's server to handle, the website was adapted to LibGuides. This was chosen as the new platform due to ease of updating and maintenance, as well as making it easier for others to update the website in emergencies.

Goals for the website remained the same. It needed to be readable, easy to use, and easy to navigate. The user base was satisfied with the previous design, so the new LibGuides version was built to mirror the website. The webmaster found that LibGuides made the website look more aesthetically pleasing and adaptable. Instead of features that had to be adjusted at the Java level, LibGuides made the IGHR website "pop" with use of large color blocks for different kinds of information. The new version also easily linked back to parts of the older website.

The LibGuides version of the IGHR site launched in December 2013. No formal usability survey was performed during the transition, but the website was tested by library faculty before launching and IGHR participants and faculty were able to provide feedback afterward. The transition was further eased by redirecting the old web address to the internal LibGuides URL.

The library upgraded to LGv2 in early 2015. This change brought necessary design changes for the IGHR site. The format remained familiar, but the look of the website was altered, and the adaptation was a process of trial and error. We needed the website to feature important information in colored boxes and LGv2 no longer had box borders. Certain features of the website, such as the "Countdown to IGHR" clock, did not move with the update and had to be reconstructed using the original HTML. The dimensions of the columns within LibGuides changed, so images made to accommodate the original measurements had to be adjusted.

CONCLUSION

SU Library has maximized its LibGuides license by employing the guides to solve a wide variety of noninstructional in-house needs. As you consider how your library might do the same, we recommend the following:

- Maximize the value of LibGuides by expanding their use beyond student study tools. Think creatively about the potential uses of LibGuides by all library faculty, staff, and other potential stakeholders.
- LibGuides are highly adaptable; leverage them to promote your university library beyond traditional services and to foster collaboration with other departments campus wide.

- Appoint an individual librarian to administrate LibGuides who will keep users informed about updates, improvements, and new ways to utilize the service.
- Think about how LibGuides can be deployed for projects and communication for library faculty and staff, and encourage new applications of LibGuides by emphasizing the product's accessibility and ease of use.

ACKNOWLEDGMENTS

The authors would like to acknowledge all contributions by SU Library LibGuide users. Without the innovative efforts of Samford Library employees, we would not have a chapter. Special thanks go to Eric Allen and Lori Northrup for allowing us to interview them.

REFERENCE

Samford University. 2015. "Quick Facts." Samford Department of Institutional Effectiveness. www.samford.edu/departments/files/Institutional_Effectiveness/Fall-2015-Quick-Facts .pdf. Accessed October 29, 2015.

VII
SYSTEM-WIDE CASE STUDY

15

Exploring How North Carolina Community College Libraries Are Using LibGuides

Suvanida Duangudom, MLS, Wake Technical Community College
Melanie Gnau, MSLS, Wake Technical Community College

LibGuides' popularity is evidenced by the growing number of users and guides being added to its user community on a daily basis. Many libraries likely subscribed with the intention of creating traditional research guides that provide users with a list of books, databases, and other resources for specific subject areas and courses. However, LibGuides has evolved into a content management system (CMS) with a multitude of uses. Libraries ideally create guides based on their users' needs, and the approach that one takes to address this may differ at other institutions. However, common themes can be found such as general information guides, faculty frequently asked questions, course guides, subject guides, and guides for information literacy, collaboration, intranet, and training. These common themes may provide other librarians with ideas to improve their own guides or address the needs of their users.

All fifty-eight community college libraries in North Carolina have an active LibGuides account, and as of fall of 2015, twenty-nine libraries had migrated to version 2 (LGv2). However, not all of these schools are using the software in the same way. We will explore how these institutions are using LibGuides to better serve the needs of their students, staff, faculty, and community—examining why and how libraries are using the system differently. Additionally, we will take a closer look at some best practices from the perspectives of a statewide consortia and community college libraries. Part of this is informed by the results of a survey that we sent out to North Carolina community college (NCCC) libraries in 2015.

LIBGUIDES IN NORTH CAROLINA

Libraries typically purchase LibGuides for their individual system or institution. NCCC libraries are unique in that our access is provided through the State Library

179

of North Carolina. The State Library contracted with Springshare, in the summer of 2012, to provide accounts for itself, NC LIVE, the eighty public library systems, and the fifty-eight community colleges in North Carolina. LibGuides volume purchasing lowered the price per institution a great deal, and this cost benefit allowed both public and community college libraries to be included in the contract. Many of the community college libraries would not have been able to afford it otherwise.

The State Library of North Carolina allowed our libraries to build a compelling online and mobile environment by providing LibGuides access for us. The platform helps libraries deploy software solutions as cost-efficient technology for hosting, management, and support of content. This is due to service being hosted on Springshare's servers, reducing the technology infrastructure and staffing needs of the libraries and increasing ease of use. It also ensures that North Carolina libraries are using the latest technologies to streamline their workflows.

Being a part of a statewide purchase had another benefit: statewide training. The State Library of North Carolina constantly offers training on how to best use LibGuides to meet the needs of our community college patrons. This is an added bonus, especially for smaller institutions that have one or two staff members, as now they have a network of experts to consult for training and one-on-one help. The State Library of North Carolina has built a guide to help facilitate training both in person and online (statelibrary.ncdcr.libguides.com/trainstation).

THE COMMUNITY COLLEGE ENVIRONMENT

There are sixty thousand LibGuides users (Springshare, Inc. 2013) from all types of libraries. Though community college libraries fall into the "academic" category, they often straddle the line between public and academic. Rural community college libraries may even serve general public patrons as often as their own students. This is due to the limited availability of their county's public library. Community colleges have their own unique challenges, which include, but are not limited to, an incredibly diverse student body, limited staffing, a rapidly changing pool of adjunct faculty, and uncertain information technology (IT) support.

The average community college student is different from her counterpart at a four-year institution. According to the American Association of Community Colleges (2015), the average age of a community college student is twenty-nine—and two-thirds of these students attend part time. However, community colleges do not only provide access for adult students. They also serve an increasing number of traditional-age and high school students who take specific courses to get ahead in their studies. In fact, half of the students who receive a baccalaureate degree attend community college at some point in the course of their undergraduate studies (American Association of Community Colleges 2015).

Community college librarians find themselves serving a multitude of roles due, in part, to both their patron base and funding. They may do instruction, reference, cataloging, collection development, and web services all in one day. Additionally, at many community college libraries in North Carolina, technical assistants outnumber librarians. Some technical assistants may find themselves performing duties that are traditionally thought to be librarian responsibilities. These include acquisitions, cataloging, and participating in reference interviews. Other technical assistants may find themselves in a more traditional role such as working the circulation desk and participating in interlibrary loan.

At the library at Martin Community College, the smallest community college in our state, the staff consists of two people: a director and an assistant. Therefore, the director must take on many of the duties commonly assigned to a librarian. Wake Technical Community College, the largest community college in our state, currently has eleven and one-fourth full-time equivalent (FTE) librarians and ten FTE library assistants—who served more than fifteen thousand FTE students across five campuses in the 2013–2014 school year (Wake Technical Community College 2015).

Communication between faculty and staff at community colleges can be challenging. The large adjunct faculty population makes it difficult for us to communicate effectively. Fifty-eight percent of faculty at U.S. community colleges are adjuncts according to a report from the Center for Community College Student Engagement (2014). This population can be even larger depending on the institution. At Davidson Community College, a rural community college that serves approximately four thousand students, adjuncts account for 71 percent of the faculty (Institute of Education Sciences 2014).

IT support can also be challenging in this environment. LibGuides users don't necessarily need to have advanced support, a web development background, or even knowledge of HTML to use the platform effectively. Limited research has been done on how IT support affects community college libraries. However, according to our survey, ease of use is the leading favorite aspect of the platform. This makes it a viable solution for the community college library environment.

LIBGUIDES SURVEY FOR NCCC LIBRARIES

Through informal conversations among librarians, at various conferences and professional development events, Wake Technical librarians began discussing the uniqueness of our system-wide consortium for LibGuides. Simultaneously, we were discussing the lack of professional literature about community college libraries. Therefore, we decided to survey community college libraries in North Carolina to discover the importance of LibGuides to these institutions. We sent this survey out to the deans or directors of all fifty-eight community college libraries, including our own, in the fall of 2015. We did this because it can be difficult to identify the LibGuides administrator at each college. If the dean or director was not the LibGuides administrator, he or she was asked to send the survey to the appropriate person.

Our survey consisted of a total of twelve questions—both qualitative and quantitative. It was kept short to encourage participation. We asked about the purpose of LibGuides at each participant's institution, their favorite aspects of the platform, challenges, and level of satisfaction. We also asked for examples of guides that they had produced. Due to the nature of this chapter, not all question results are provided. Thirty-six (62 percent) of the fifty-eight community colleges responded to confirm that they were using LibGuides. We received an addition five responses (9 percent) from institutions where, although the platform was activated, it was not being used. They explained that it was not being used due to limited time and staff. We did not receive a response from seventeen libraries (29 percent).

Most respondents had been using LibGuides for two to four years, and individual guides were created primarily by librarians. Purpose, however, varied widely. Most schools were using LibGuides for instruction, research guides, reader's advisory, and marketing/events. Notably, approximately 20 percent of respondents were also using LibGuides as their primary website or library homepage.

Ease of Use and Challenges

Libraries responded favorably to many aspects of LibGuides. Ease of use was the most common response. This was followed closely by the ability to reuse content. Challenges most frequently reported included compliance with the Americans with Disabilities Act (ADA) and upkeep/time issues. Despite these challenges, 70 percent of libraries reported a satisfaction rating of four on a scale of one (lowest) to five (highest). Ease of use was primarily responsible for the favorable satisfaction rating.

Regarding ease of use, LibGuides allows librarians and staff to be less dependent on web developers or IT at their institutions. Mary Anne Caudle at Martin Community College explains:

> When I came here, the library website had incorrect hours, lacked links to all of our databases, had no contact information for the library and was generally not very helpful. There was no web master at that point and no hope of getting changes made any time soon. LibGuides allowed me to correct all of the above quickly and also put in features that help students find the information they need, all from one point of access. (Mary Anne Caudle, survey response to authors, September 18, 2015)

Grant LeFoe at South Piedmont Community College echoed those thoughts:

> The easy-to-use platform makes it far more effective to customize each page and embed images, video, and search boxes to make the pages more interactive and functional for the students. We just find the look of LibGuides to be cleaner than our library website and now host many of the library website's subpages on LibGuides. (Grant LeFoe, survey response to authors, September 17, 2015)

Instruction

Some community college libraries use LibGuides as a platform for instruction. Rachel McLean from Tri-County Community College wrote, "In the past, I would teach with traditional PowerPoint presentations. Now, I use the LibGuide to aid in the instruction session. With LibGuides, I can organize electronic library resources easily and quickly" (Rachel McLean, survey response to authors, September 30, 2015). Staci Wilson from Catawba Valley Community College concurs: "[Lib-Guides] are wonderfully flexible tools that allow us to offer instruction from a distance, act as learning object repositories (tailored to specific classes), or work in place of PowerPoint presentations in the face-to-face context" (Staci Wilson, survey response to authors, October 5, 2015).

Common Problems

NCCC library staff are generally satisfied with LibGuides. However, some respondents identified issues with the platform. ADA compliance was a challenge indicated by 75 percent of those surveyed. Alison Beard from Caldwell Community College and Technical Institute suggested that Springshare should create built-in software to test for ADA compliance (Alison Beard, survey response to authors, October 5, 2015).

Upkeep was the second most common complaint. However, we received no suggestions for improvement in this area. We believe that this challenge may be due, in part, to time commitments. Limited time closely followed upkeep as a challenging aspect of LibGuides—58 percent of survey respondents stated that it was a problem for them. Limited time, due to a small staff, was also cited as an issue for those who did not currently use LibGuides.

Respondents suggested improvements when asked "If given the choice, what would you change about LibGuides?" The main theme that emerged was desire for a more flexible interface. Six respondents specifically addressed guide layout in this context. Alan Unsworth at Surry Community College explains:

> [I wish LibGuides had] more customization options for free, like being able to create a "box" without a title or change around the column numbers on different rows. The look is clean but is also very canned and it's difficult to make LibGuides look unique. It would be nice if LibGuides offered free or cheap "themes" like WordPress where you could pick different looks and feels and have full control over the layout options. (Alan Unsworth, survey response to authors, October 5, 2015)

"BEST OF" LIBGUIDES EXAMPLES FROM NCCC LIBRARIES

Let's take a closer look at some "best of" examples we've identified among community college libraries in North Carolina. These were selected to demonstrate how libraries are best addressing the needs and challenges unique to their institutions. Each featured "best of" example features a brief description of the guide, a URL link to it, and (when possible) an image of the guide.

Examples are from both large and small libraries within the NCCC system that are using LibGuides for research guides, promotional tools, instructional handouts, staff training, a collaborative platform, intranet/internal communication, and/or as a library website. These categories are being used because the majority of our respondents indicated that LibGuides has vastly improved their online presence in these ways.

Subject, Course, and Information Literacy Guides

Subject guides point users to the best resources (e.g., books, articles, and websites) available for a specific subject area. The Air Conditioning, Heating & Refrigeration guide (researchguides.cpcc.edu/ahr) by Denise Keating at Central Piedmont Community College features an applied technologies subject area that is unique to the community college setting. She does an excellent job of highlighting a variety of resources that can be found in this area.

Course guides are often created in collaboration with faculty for a specific course or assignment. Working with faculty on layout and content customization helps to fit the needs of the course and/or assignment. Angela Davis at Pitt Community College has created an English 112 class guide with a clean, aesthetically pleasing design that utilizes top level tabs (libguides.pittcc.edu/eng112/oryx).

LibGuides is also used as an information literacy instruction tool. Creating guides specifically for each instructional class, instead of providing students with numerous handouts, makes for a great teaching tool. This guide created by Mary Gomez at Rockingham Community College is an excellent example—it is instructional, informative, and engaging to the audience (rockinghamcc.libguides.com/zombies). She also does a great job in using the guide to promote the library's collections. Figure 15.1 shows a glimpse of this creative guide as it looked at the time of writing.

Marketing and Highlighting Resources

Promotion and marketing plays a key role in communicating with library patrons about new collections, services, and resources that are available to them. However, there is not a set budget for promotions and marketing at many community college libraries. Therefore, libraries need to seek free or low-cost alternatives—or use existing tools to market to their patrons. For example, at Surry Community College, Alan Unsworth has created a nice guide that highlights the library's newly acquired books and DVDs (library.surry.edu/new).

Additionally, depending on where the college is located and its target audience, some guides may promote special collections. Julie Humphrey at Durham Tech Community College has created a graphic novel guide that defines graphic novels and also includes resources for children, teens, and adults (durhamtech.libguides. com/graphicnovels). Similarly, Wake Technical Community College has created a guide to target a specific audience—early college students—with a young adult materials guide (libguides.waketech.edu/YA).

Some libraries choose to feature all of their resources on one page. Heather Cyre at Haywood Community College created a guide to "consolidate all our resources we

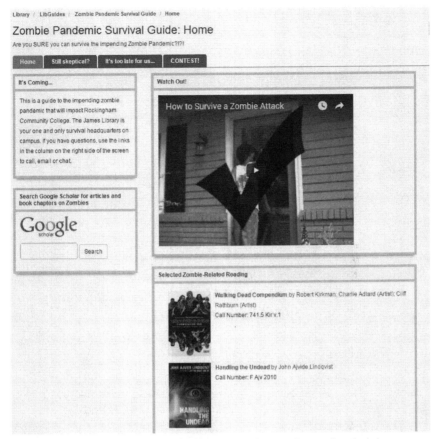

Figure 15.1.   Using LibGuides as an information literacy instructional tool to engage the audience and promote the library's collections.

subscribe to outside of NC LIVE into one location. Previously these items were scattered throughout library web pages and became overwhelming for students to track down" (Heather Cyre, survey response to authors, October 5, 2015). This guide can be viewed at haywood.libguides.com/e_resources.

LibGuides as a Collaborative Platform

Many libraries are turning to LibGuides as a platform due to limited budgets, the need for reusable content, and the need for more control of their website. Some even use it as a collaborative tool to share conference materials and professional development resources with colleagues locally and/or at other institutions. The North Carolina Community College Libraries Association (NCCCLA), for example, has used LibGuides as its conference website for the past few years (libguides.waketech.edu/NCCCLA2015). This allows organizers to easily offer information about reg-

Figure 15.2. Using LibGuides as an online collaborative platform to share professional development materials or networking with colleagues.

istration, lodging, and sessions and even to share follow-up presentation materials. The conference website, at the time of writing, is depicted in figure 15.2.

At Wake Technical Community College we have created an internal, staff-only guide (libguides.waketech.edu/intranet) to share information such as policies, procedures, best practices, how-to tips, and professional development notes. This guide is helpful for new employee orientations and provides easy access to information at point of need. Guides of this type can be marked as private or password-protected in order to limit access. An example is provided in figure 15.3.

Figure 15.3. Using LibGuides to create internal library staff-only guides to share policies and procedures specific to an institution (based on survey responses from North Carolina community colleges libraries).

LibGuides as a Library Website

Twenty percent of those surveyed indicated that they use LibGuides as their library website. This is not surprising; websites built using this platform provide librarians with an easy way to manage their public image without having an extensive background in HTML. Websites built using LibGuides also provide a way to update, store, and reuse content in real time. This means that you do not have to depend on other departments, such as IT, to do it for you. An example of one such LibGuides-based library website, for Craven Community College library, can be found at cravencc.libguides.com/library.

CONCLUSION

LibGuides has become an essential part of NCCC libraries services. Librarians have found freedom from the constraints of coding and a CMS that meets their diverse needs. Although problems such as ADA compliance, upkeep, and time constraints still remain, the majority of North Carolina library staff members are satisfied with the platform. Many librarians have even developed out-of-the-box ideas into creative, engaging guides. These go beyond the traditional research guide; they include twenty-first-century content that addresses our community colleges' diverse information needs.

REFERENCES

American Association of Community Colleges. 2015. "Students at Community Colleges." www.aacc.nche.edu/AboutCC/Trends/Pages/studentsatcommunitycolleges.aspx.

Center for Community College Student Engagement. 2014. "Contingent Commitments: Bringing Part Time Faculty into Focus." www.ccsse.org/docs/PTF_Special_Report.pdf.

Institute of Education Sciences. 2014. "College Navigator: Davidson Community College." National Center for Education Statistics. nces.ed.gov/collegenavigator/?id=198376#general.

Springshare, Inc. 2013. "LibGuides by Springshare." www.springshare.com/libguides/.

Wake Technical Community College. 2015. "2013–2014 Fact Book." www.waketech.edu/sites/default/files/ieandresearch/2013Factbook/2013-2014_Fact_Book_Final.pdf.

Index

About the Editors and Contributors

Ryan L. Sittler, PhD, is an associate professor and instructional technology/information literacy librarian at California University of Pennsylvania. He holds a PhD in communications media and instructional technology from Indiana University of Pennsylvania, and his research interests are in information literacy and educational media design for learning and performance improvement. Previous publication topics include instructional technology as it applies to librarians, information literacy teaching and learning, and LibGuides utilization. Ryan can be contacted via e-mail at sittler@calu.edu or via Twitter: @ryanlsittler.

Aaron W. Dobbs is an associate professor and scholarly communication and electronic resources librarian at Shippensburg University of Pennsylvania. Aaron manages the library website, fully managed in LibGuides, and lives in the future as often as possible. His previous publication and presentation topics include LibGuides, web design, future planning, and library assessment. His current research areas include library assessment and anticipating future users' research skills, needs, and background assumptions. Aaron can be contacted via e-mail at aaron@thelibrarian.org and via Twitter: @awd.

* * *

Christy Allen is the assistant director for discovery services for the Furman University Libraries.

Cody Behles is the emerging technologies librarian for the University of Memphis Libraries.

Jason Bengston is the assistant director, Library Information Technology Services, for Kansas State University. An experienced, full-stack web developer, Jason builds projects using a wide variety of languages and data models. His work may be seen in journals such as *Library Hi-Tech* and *The Journal of Hospital Librarianship*.

Albert Bertram is a lead developer at the University of Michigan Library. He is responsible for maintaining the architecture for the library's website and the library's integration with the University of Michigan's learning management systems. Albert received a master's degree in computational linguistics from the University of Washington and has contributed to a variety of open source projects such as Nmh (www .nongnu.org/nmh/), JGroups (jgroups.org), and Hydra (projecthydra.org).

Brigitte Billeaudeaux is a library assistant II in the Department of Preservation and Special Collections at the University of Memphis Libraries. She manages the department's digital projects, helps coordinate and curate cross-departmental exhibitions, and works to create interactive online experiences using the libraries' special collections. She has more than ten years of experience working in cultural heritage institutions and museums in Memphis, Tennessee, and the Mid-South. She holds a master's degree in Anthropology from the University of Memphis as well as a master's of information sciences degree from the University of Tennessee at Knoxville. She can be contacted at bbilledx@memphis.edu.

Lisa Campbell is digital learning services librarian at the University of Michigan Library, where she oversees several reference and instruction-related technologies (including LibGuides) and coordinates large-scale web content improvement projects. She received a master's degree from the University of Pittsburgh's School of Information Sciences and a bachelor's of fine arts from Carnegie Mellon University. In her publications and presentations, Lisa explores the interconnectedness of technology and public services. Her other publications regarding Springshare products include *LibAnswers: Improving Asynchronous Service* (2012).

Susan K. Cavanaugh, MS, MPH, is currently the assistant director of the Medical Library at Cooper Medical School of Rowan University. Ms. Cavanaugh received a master's of science from the College of Information Science and Technology, Drexel University in 1995, but has worked in medical libraries for more than thirty years. In 2007 she earned a master's of public health from the School of Public Health, Drexel University. Ms. Cavanaugh also holds a faculty appointment in the Department of Biomedical Sciences at CMSRU. She is a co-course director of the Scholars Workshop course, collaborates with Dean Paul Katz to teach a course on the Social Mission of Medical Schools, and is a core faculty contributor to the Life Stages course. She is currently pursuing a doctorate in public affairs with an emphasis on community development, at Rutgers University–Camden Campus.

Melissa Cornwell is the distance learning librarian at the Kreitzberg Library at Norwich University. She has a BA in English from Southern Illinois University and an MLIS from the University of Illinois.

Alice L. Daugherty, MLIS, is the collections assessment and analysis librarian at Louisiana State University Libraries. She has worked at LSU Libraries since 2004 and currently serves as the point person for assessment and statistics within the libraries. She has been very active in ALA, having served on the ACRL Value of Academic Libraries Committee, on the ACRL Task Force on Assessment Competencies, and multiple committee appointments within the Distance Learning Section, where she is currently the section's past-chair.

Jane C. Daugherty is the user engagement librarian at Samford University Library. In addition to providing instruction and research assistance for Samford students and faculty, Jane manages the library's social media and student outreach. She received her MLIS from the University of Alabama.

Lance Day is a reference and research services Librarian at Samford University Library. He is the LibGuides administrator, provides instruction, and is the liaison to the Physical Therapy and Social Work Departments. Lance received an MLIS from the University of Alabama and an MSW from the University of Georgia.

Meghan L. Dowell, consulting librarian at Beloit College, specializes in critical library instruction, campus engagement, and data literacy. She holds an MLIS from Long Island University's Palmer School of Library and Information Science (2012) and a BS in economics from Portland State University (2010). She would like to thank her fellow Beloit College librarians and instructional technologist Jedidiah Rex.

Suvanida Duangudom is the campus librarian at Wake Technical Community College, Northern Wake Campus. She serves as a LibGuides administrator for Wake Tech Libraries and provides staff training. Additionally, she conducts workshops and provides training to library staff at other community colleges and public libraries on LibGuides and LibCal through her work with the State Library of North Carolina. She is currently serving as the community college representative on the NC LIVE Librarians Council and NCLA Technology and Trends executive committee. She has also published several book reviews for the North Carolina Libraries Association.

David Dunaway is the science librarian at Louisiana State University in Baton Rouge, Louisiana. He received his master's degree in library and information science, master's degree in secondary science education, and bachelor's of science in chemistry from Louisiana State University.

Jamie L. Emery is a research and instruction librarian and associate professor at Saint Louis University. She received her MS in library and information science from the University of Illinois at Urbana-Champaign. She is the author of "The Expanding Role of Information Literacy in the Freshman Writing Program at Saint Louis University: A Case Study," which appeared in the book *Curriculum-Based Library Instruction: From Cultivating Faculty Relationships to Assessment* (2014). Her research interests include data-driven LibGuides design, information literacy instruction, and social media. She can be contacted at jemery2@slu.edu.

Sarah E. Fancher is a research and instruction librarian and associate professor at Saint Louis University. She received her MS in library and information science from the University of Illinois at Urbana-Champaign. She is a frequent reviewer for *Choice*. Her research interests include library marketing, business information literacy, and distance librarianship. She can be contacted at sfancher@slu.edu.

Angela R. Flenner, MLIS, MSHP, is the systems librarian at College of Charleston Libraries. She is interested in interoperability of data among proprietary and open-source systems and using metadata to improve access and preservation of library resources. Correspondence may be directed to flennera@cofc.edu.

Melanie Gnau is the instruction librarian at Wake Technical Community College, Northern Wake Campus. She serves as a LibGuides administrator for Wake Tech Libraries. She provides staff training on LibGuides for Wake Tech staff, as well as NC library staff. Additionally, she serves as North Carolina Community College Library Association president and is a current member of the Website Advisory Committee (WAC) for NC LIVE.

Jeremy Hall is a graduate of Florida State University's School of Library and Information Studies with graduate certificates in web design and information architecture. Jeremy worked as a professional soldier, teacher, stockbroker, and loan officer before initially settling into public and finally academic libraries. Jeremy can now be found working with code, customizing Springshare products, and developing and improving virtual systems at the University of North Florida, where he serves as the virtual services librarian.

Andrea Hebert is the human sciences, education, and distance learning librarian at Louisiana State University. She serves as the liaison to the Schools of Education, Kinesiology, Social Work, Human Resource Education and Workforce Development, and Library and Information Science as well as the distance learning programs. She received a BA in English and Latin from Louisiana State University, an MA in Latin from the University of Georgia, and an MLIS from Louisiana State University.

Catherine Marchetta is a second-year medical student at Cooper Medical School of Rowan University. Ms. Marchetta served as the MEDAcademy coordinator. Ms. Marchetta graduated with a bachelor's degree in biological science and Italian studies from Wellesley College.

Lauren Newton is the head of instruction at the University of North Florida's Thomas G. Carpenter Library. Before earning her MLIS, she earned a BA in history. She enjoys learning and teaching and looks forward to the challenges of meeting the library instruction needs of today's learners. Lauren is especially interested in innovative methods of conducting library instruction both face-to-face and online. Most recently, Lauren has been integrating active learning methods to enhance the engagement of learners with the research process. She has found that these methods are particularly suited to a flipped-classroom style that allows learners to practice information literacy concepts and skills.

Amanda Peach is a reference and instruction librarian at Berea College, a private liberal arts school in Berea, Kentucky, which is known for its unique status as a labor college. Amanda's library passions are one-on-one reference consultations because of the personal connections they foster with students and supervising student reference workers because of all of the many varied ways they teach her to approach the world and research. She received her MLIS from the University of Kentucky and an MA in higher education administration from the University of Louisville.

Christa E. Poparad, MSLIS, is the head of Research and Instruction Services in Addlestone Library at the College of Charleston. Research interests include scaffolding information literacy instruction throughout the curriculum, providing research and computing services to diverse user communities, and practical assessment of library resources and services. Correspondence may be directed to poparadce@cofc.edu.

Scott Salzman is the web discovery librarian for the Furman University Libraries.

Jennifer Schnabel, MA, MLIS, is currently the English librarian at The Ohio State University. She previously worked as the assistant to the dean for community engagement at the University of Memphis Libraries. She has more than ten years of experience in higher education, including teaching reading, writing, and English literature courses, and has held several public relations and marketing positions in nonprofit and cultural institutions in Philadelphia. She can be reached at schnabel.23@osu.edu.

Ken Varnum is the senior program manager for discovery, delivery, and learning analytics at the University of Michigan Library. In this role, Ken is responsible for the library's discovery and delivery interfaces and the library's evolving learning analytics infrastructure. He received a master's degree from the University of Michigan's School of Information and his bachelor's of arts from Grinnell College. A frequent speaker and author, Ken speaks and writes about analytics, discovery, and content management. In addition to numerous articles and chapters, he wrote *Drupal in Libraries* (2012), compiled the LITA Guide *The Top Technologies Every Librarian Needs to Know* (2014), and edited Lorcan Dempsey's *The Network Reshapes the Library* (2014). His next book, *Exploring Discovery: The Front Door to a Library's Licensed and*

Digitized Content, is to be published by ALA Editions in 2016. He blogs at rss4lib. com and can be found on Twitter at @varnum.

Carla T. Waddell is the government documents librarian and the chair of Reference and Research Services at Samford University Library. She began her library career as an instruction/reference librarian when HTML was needed to create research guides. Imagine her joy when she discovered LibGuides. She received her MLIS from the University of Alabama.

Stephanie M. Lee Weiss is the online learning librarian at the University of North Florida's Thomas G. Carpenter Library. She earned a BA in Spanish and an MS LIS. Stephanie has a passion for making connections, which helps make her a natural learner and teacher. Before becoming a librarian, she worked for more than five years in adult education, training, and professional development and also taught in the K–12 arena. She is an advocate for online and distance learning and is intrigued by the possibilities that digital scholarship offers to seekers of information, whether for personal gratification or school.

Sharon Whitfield is the emerging technologies librarian at Cooper Medical School of Rowan University. Ms. Whitfield has obtained her MLIS from the University of Pittsburgh and is pursuing an EdD in educational leadership from Rowan University. Her research interests include using technology to improve user access, studying goal-orientated user behavior, and using wearable and beacon technologies to expand the concept of library as a place.

Lydia Willoughby is a research and education librarian at the Sojourner Truth Library at the State University of New York (SUNY) at New Paltz. Willoughby's pedagogy and scholarship address critical theory, multimodal digital learning, and gamification in education. Prior to New Paltz, she was the visiting assistant librarian at SUNY Plattsburgh and managed online integration of library resources (2013–2015). Willoughby earned an MLIS from Long Island University (2011) and an MA in English literature from the University of Montana (2006) and is a graduate of Bard College (2003). In 2013, Willoughby was selected as one of *Library Journal*'s "Movers & Shakers" in the community builder category for her advocacy with rural libraries.

Lauren M. Young is instruction coordinator/reference and research services librarian at Samford University Library. Her library career has seen equal time spent in technical services and public services roles, and she specializes in serving the information needs of health sciences programs and patrons. Lauren earned her MLIS from the University of Southern Mississippi and her MA in English from the University of Mississippi, and she is a senior member of the Academy of Health Information Professionals.